Basic Color Terms

BASIC COLOR TERMS
Their Universality and Evolution

BRENT BERLIN AND PAUL KAY

THE DAVID HUME SERIES
PHILOSOPHY AND COGNITIVE SCIENCE REISSUES

 CSLI PUBLICATIONS

For two colorful ladies
EAB *and* PBK

Copyright © 1999
CSLI Publications
Center for the Study of Language and Information
Leland Stanford Junior University
Printed in the United States
03 02 01 00   2 3 4 5

Library of Congress Cataloging-in-Publication Data

Berlin, Brent.
Basic color terms : their universality and evolution / Brent Berlin and Paul Kay.
p.   cm. – (David Hume series)
Originally published: Berkeley : University of California Press, 1991. Paperback ed.
Includes bibliographical references (p.   ) and index.

ISBN 1-57586-162-3 (alk. paper)

1. Colors, Words for. 2. Polyglot glossaries, phrase books, etc.
I. Kay, Paul, 1934–   . II. Title.
P341.B4 1999
401'.43–dc21   99-12619
CIP

∞ The acid-free paper used in this book meets the minimum requirements of the
American National Standard for Information Sciences – Permanence of Paper for
Printed Library Materials, ANSI Z39.48-1984.

The David Hume Series of Philosophy and Cognitive Science Reissues consists of
previously published works that are important and useful to scholars and students
working in the area of cognitive science. The aim of the series is to keep these
indispensable works in print in affordable paperback editions.

In addition to this series, CSLI Publications also publishes lecture notes, monographs,
working papers, and conference proceedings. Our aim is to make new results, ideas,
and approaches available as quickly as possible. Please visit our web site at
http://csli-publications.stanford.edu/
for comments on this and other titles, as well as for changes and corrections by the
author and publisher.

Preface to the Paperback Edition

THE present text represents without change the original 1969 edition of this work. The volume of research that has taken place in the area of basic color terms in the past two decades has rendered it unfeasible for us to revise the original text for this reprinting. This volume does, however, contain the addition of a comprehensive bibliography, compiled by Luisa Maffi, of the research on basic color terms since 1969. That bibliography also includes the more important modern sources from the period before the original publication of this work.

Research on basic color terms since 1969 has led to a succession of revisions of the evolutionary sequence according to which basic color vocabularies grow (see, for example, Berlin and Berlin 1975; Kay 1975; Kay and McDaniel 1978; Berlin, Kay, and Merrifield 1986; Kay, Berlin, and Merrifield 1991). While the accumulation of new data has brought substantial changes to our view of the details of the developmental sequence as originally represented in this text, the two principal findings of the original study, here reprinted, have stood the test of these new data: (1) there are substantive universal constraints on the shape of basic color lexicons —systems of color naming do not vary randomly or capriciously across languages but are constrained to a small number of possible types; and (2) basic color lexicons change type over time by adding basic color terms in a highly constrained, though not mechanically predictable, manner.

Much has been discovered since 1969 regarding the psychophysical and neurophysiological determinants of universal, cross-linguistic constraints on the shape of basic color lexicons, and something, albeit less, can now also be said with some confidence regarding the constraining effects of these language-independent processes of color perception and conceptualization on the direction of evolution of basic color term lexicons (see particularly Kay and McDaniel 1978; Kay, Berlin, and Merrifield 1991. The literature referred to in Luisa Maffi's bibliography should be consulted for further detail regarding subsequent developments in the expansion, detailed specification, and interrelation of findings (1) and (2) of this original study).

Currently, we are engaged, in collaboration with William Merrifield, in a survey of the basic color lexicons of over one hundred unwritten languages from around the world, the data being gathered in each native language, *in situ*, from a large number of native language consultants who are insofar as possible monolingual. The World Color Survey is sponsored by the National Science Foundation, the Summer Institute of Linguistics, and the University of California at Berkeley. It is our hope that eventual publication of the results of that survey will further deepen our understanding of the semantic universals and constrained evolutionary trajectories embodied in systems of basic color terms.

B.B., P.K.
Berkeley
June 1991

Preface

THE work reported in this monograph was begun in the winter of 1967 in a graduate seminar at Berkeley. Many of the basic data were gathered by members of the seminar and the theoretical framework presented here was initially developed in the context of the seminar discussions. We are indebted to the members of that seminar, both for their contributions to the method and theory of the study and for the data they contributed. These members were Christopher Corson (Catalan, Pomo), Sylvia Forman (Bulgarian, Thai), Keith Kernan, Paul Madarasz (Hungarian, Indonesian, Mandarin, Korean, Swahili, Vietnamese), Erica McClure (Mandarin, Japanese), Peter Steager (Japanese), Brian Stross (Cantonese, Spanish), and Kathleen MacLaren Zaretsky (Hebrew, Urdu). We would like also to thank Charles O. Frake for the Tagalog materials and Elaine Kaufman for the Ibibio data. The authors are responsible for data on Arabic, English, and Tzeltal.

We are grateful to the following individuals, who have provided data and comments in the form of personal communications: Haruo Aoki (Nez Perce), Keith Basso (Western Apache), Denzel Carr (Malay), Elizabeth Colson (Tonga), Osama A. Doumani (Lebanese Arabic), Mary Foster (Tarascan, Sierra Popoluca), William H. Geoghegan (Samal), N. H. H. Graburn (Eskimo), Kenneth Hale (Papago), Don Bahr (Papago), Terrence Kaufman (Chinook Jargon), K.-F. Koch (Jalé), Richard Lee (!Kung Bushman), Eugene Ogan (Nasioi), Dan I. Slobin (Russian).

We have received many useful comments and suggestions on earlier versions of the manuscript and on verbal presentations of this material. We would like to express appreciation for these to Robert Ascher, Robbins Burling, Wallace L. Chafe, Michael D. Coe, Harold C. Conklin, George L. Cowgill, Roy G. D'Andrade, A. Richard Diebold, Jr., Phoebe Diebold, Marshall E. Durbin, Susan Ervin-Tripp, Charles O. Frake, William H. Geoghegan, Joseph H. Greenberg, John J. Gumperz, Karl Heider, Nicholas A. Hopkins, Terrence S. Kaufman, Herbert Landar, Jean Lave, Richard Lee, Floyd G. Lounsbury, Barbara MacRoberts, Duane G. Metzger, June Nash, Eugene Ogan, Douglas L. Oliver, Patricia Porth, John M. Roberts, A. Kimball Romney, David M. Schneider, T. A. Sebeok, Dan I. Slobin, the late Morris Swadesh, and Stephen A. Tyler.

We would like also to thank many of our colleagues and students in the Departments of Anthropology, Linguistics and Psychology at Berkeley for helpful comments and suggestions.

For particularly detailed comments, we owe special gratitude to Katherine Branstetter, Edwin E. Cook, Christopher Day, David Day, John L. Fischer, Barbara Heiman, Michael Heiman, Del H. Hymes, Ron Kaplan, Angela Little and Rosslyn Suchman.

The extremely able research assistance of Katherine Branstetter, Barbara Heiman, and Malcolm McClure has been invaluable. We are also grateful for assistance in various phases of the study to Catherine Brandel, Barbara Gullahorn, Rachel Holmen, and Nancy Papalexis.

We have further benefitted from seminar discussion throughout winter and spring 1968 with Katherine Branstetter, Barbara Heiman, Michael Heiman, and Ron Kaplan.

Jill Varney, Haydee Vives and others are due heartfelt thanks for typing and re-typing of the manuscript, and Jeanbelle Rosenman for editing and indexing.

No attempt has been made to employ a uniform orthography throughout. Native forms have been cited in the orthography of the source document. In general, the spellings are sufficiently accurate for identification at morphemic and lexical levels but should not be relied on for phonological purposes. The heterogeneity of sources as well as the age of some of these, along with the diversity of major stocks and individual languages involved, have enforced this somewhat cavalier attitude toward orthography. We would have preferred to employ a standard orthography throughout but to do so would have required a major research effort for which resources were not available. We have, however, used standard orthographies for the twenty languages on which we have gathered original data. The authorities used for standard orthographies are listed in Appendix IV.

The complete set of color chips used in the construction of the stimulus board was obtained from the Munsell Color Company, 2441 North Calvert Street, Baltimore, Maryland, 21218.

B. B., P. K.
August, 1968

Contents

Tables

Figures

Basic Color Terms

INTRODUCTION

ETHNOSCIENCE studies, and studies of color vocabulary in particular, have firmly established that to understand the full range of meaning of a word in any language, each new language must be approached in its own terms, without *a priori* theories of semantic universals. H. C. Conklin (1955) has shown, for example, that Hanunóo "color" words in fact encode a great deal of non-colorimetric information. The essentially methodological point made in such studies has been frequently misinterpreted by anthropologists and linguists as an argument against the existence of semantic universals. The research reported here strongly indicates that semantic universals do exist in the domain of color vocabulary. Moreover, these universals appear to be related to the historical development of all languages in a way that can properly be termed evolutionary.

§ 1 THE DATA, HYPOTHESIS, AND GENERAL FINDINGS

The primary experimental data were collected by students and the authors from native-speaking informants in each of twenty languages from a number of unrelated language families. These materials were supplemented by comparative data from whatever writings we could find, bringing our present sample of languages to ninety-eight, representing a wide variety of major linguistic stocks.

The study was originally designed as an experimental test of the following, loosely stated, hypothesis. The prevailing doctrine of American linguists and anthropologists has, in this century, been that of extreme linguistic relativity. Briefly, the doctrine of extreme linguistic relativity holds that each language performs the coding of experience into sound in a unique manner. Hence, each language is semantically arbitrary relative to every other language. According to this view, the search for semantic universals is fruitless in principle. The doctrine is chiefly associated in America with the names of Edward Sapir and B. L. Whorf. Proponents of this view frequently offer as a paradigm example the alleged total semantic arbitrariness of the lexical coding of color.[1] We suspect that this allegation of total arbitrariness in the way languages segment the color space is a gross overstatement.

Our hypothesis was based on our intuitive experience in several languages of three unrelated major stocks. Our feeling was that color words translate too easily among various pairs of unrelated languages for the extreme linguistic relativity thesis to be valid. Our results support the hypothesis and cast doubt on the commonly held belief that each language segments the three-dimensional color continuum arbitrarily and independently of each other language.[2] It appears now that, although different languages encode in their vocabularies different *numbers* of basic color categories, a total universal inventory of exactly eleven basic color categories exists from which the eleven or fewer basic color terms of any given language are always drawn. The eleven basic color categories are *white, black, red, green, yellow, blue, brown, purple, pink, orange,* and *grey*.

A second and totally unexpected finding is the following. If a language encodes fewer than eleven basic color categories, then there are strict limitations on which categories it may encode. The distributional restrictions of color terms across languages are:

1. All languages contain terms for white and black.
2. If a language contains three terms, then it contains a term for red.
3. If a language contains four terms, then it contains a term for either green or yellow (but not both) .
4. If a language contains five terms, then it contains terms for both green and yellow.

5. If a language contains six terms, then it contains a term for blue.

6. If a language contains seven terms, then it contains a term for brown.

7. If a language contains eight or more terms, then it contains a term for purple, pink, orange, grey, or some combination of these.

These distributional facts are summarized in Table I, in which each row corresponds to an actually occurring type of

TABLE I

THE TWENTY-TWO ACTUALLY OCCURRING TYPES
OF BASIC COLOR LEXICON

Type	No. of basic color terms	white	black	red	green	yellow	blue	brown	pink	purple	orange	grey
		Perceptual categories encoded in the basic color terms										
1	2	+	+	−	−	−	−	−	−	−	−	−
2	3	+	+	+	−	−	−	−	−	−	−	−
3	4	+	+	+	+	−	−	−	−	−	−	−
4	4	+	+	+	−	+	−	−	−	−	−	−
5	5	+	+	+	+	+	−	−	−	−	−	−
6	6	+	+	+	+	+	+	−	−	−	−	−
7	7	+	+	+	+	+	+	+	−	−	−	−
8	8	+	+	+	+	+	+	+	+	−	−	−
9	8	+	+	+	+	+	+	+	−	+	−	−
10	8	+	+	+	+	+	+	+	−	−	+	−
11	8	+	+	+	+	+	+	+	−	−	−	+
12	9	+	+	+	+	+	+	+	+	+	−	−
13	9	+	+	+	+	+	+	+	+	−	+	−
14	9	+	+	+	+	+	+	+	+	−	−	+
15	9	+	+	+	+	+	+	+	−	+	+	−
16	9	+	+	+	+	+	+	+	−	+	−	+
17	9	+	+	+	+	+	+	+	−	−	+	+
18	10	+	+	+	+	+	+	+	+	+	+	−
19	10	+	+	+	+	+	+	+	+	+	−	+
20	10	+	+	+	+	+	+	+	+	−	+	+
21	10	+	+	+	+	+	+	+	−	+	+	+
22	11	+	+	+	+	+	+	+	+	+	+	+

NOTE: Only these twenty-two out of the logically possible 2,048 combinations of the eleven basic color categories are found.

basic color lexicon. The pattern displayed by the actual distribution is a tight one; of the 2,048 (that is, 2^{11}) possible combinations of the eleven basic color terms, just twenty-two, about 1 per cent, are found to occur in fact.

Moreover, the twenty-two types which do occur are not unrelated but may be summarized by (or generated from) a rather simple rule:

$$(1) \quad \begin{bmatrix} white \\ black \end{bmatrix} < [red] < \begin{bmatrix} green \\ yellow \end{bmatrix} < [blue] < [brown] < \begin{bmatrix} purple \\ pink \\ orange \\ grey \end{bmatrix}$$

where, for distinct color categories (a, b), the expression $a < b$ signifies that a is present in every language in which b is present and also in some language in which b is not present. Rule (1) is thus a partial order on the set of basic color categories, the six bracketed sets being a series of six equivalence classes of this order.

It is argued in § 2 that rule (1) represents not only a distributional statement for contemporary languages but also the chronological order of the lexical encoding of basic color categories in each language. The chronological order is in turn interpreted as a sequence of evolutionary stages.

In §§ 2 and 3, additional data are adduced which show that the six equivalence classes of (1) correspond to seven temporal-evolutionary stages. In particular, the class [green, yellow] corresponds to the third and fourth stages rather than to a single stage as might be surmised from the data presented so far. The logical, partial ordering of rule (1) thus corresponds, according to our hypothesis, to a temporal-evolutionary ordering, as follows:

$$(2) \quad \begin{bmatrix} white \\ black \end{bmatrix} \rightarrow [red] \begin{array}{c} \nearrow [green] \rightarrow [yellow] \searrow \\ \searrow [yellow] \rightarrow [green] \nearrow \end{array} [blue] \rightarrow [brown] \rightarrow \begin{bmatrix} purple \\ pink \\ orange \\ grey \end{bmatrix}$$

where the meaning of the arrow will be discussed in § 2.

In sum, our two major findings indicate that the referents for the basic color terms of all languages appear to be drawn from a set of eleven universal perceptual categories, and these categories become encoded in the history of a given language in a partially fixed order. There appears to be no evidence to indicate that differences in complexity of basic color lexicons between one language and another reflect perceptual differences between the speakers of those languages.

§ *1.1 Procedure*

Standardized color stimuli were used in conducting the research. These consist of a set of 329 color chips provided by the Munsell Color Company. The set is composed of 320 color chips of forty equally spaced hues and eight degrees of brightness, all at maximum saturation, and nine chips of neutral hue (white, black and greys). The full set of chips was mounted on stiff cardboard and covered with clear acetate to form the array shown in Figure 1. With the exception of our addition of the neutral hue series, these materials are the same as those used by Lenneberg and Roberts (1956) in their classic cross-cultural study of English and Zuni color terminology.[3] Our method of eliciting basic color terms and obtaining the individual mappings differs, however, from theirs, as may be seen by comparing the following discussion with their work (see § 3.7).

The data were gathered in two stages. First, the basic color words of the language in question were elicited from the informant, using as little as possible of any other language.[4] Secondly, each subject was instructed to map both the focal point and the outer boundary of each of his basic color terms on the array of standard color stimuli described above.

§ *1.2 Defining the concept of basic color term*

Every language has an indefinitely large number of expressions that denote the sensation of color. Note, for example, the following English expressions: (a) *crimson,* (b) *scarlet,* (c) *blond,* (d) *blue-green,* (e) *bluish,* (f) *lemon-colored,* (g) *salmon-colored,* (h) *the color of the rust on my aunt's old Chevrolet.* But psychologists, linguists, and anthropologists have long operated with a concept of basic color term, or basic color word, which excludes forms such as (a) – (h) and includes forms like *black, white, red,* and *green.* However, the expression basic color term does not have a unique operational definition. We used the following procedure for the determination of basic color terms. Ideally, each basic color term should exhibit the following four characteristics:

(i) It is *monolexemic;* that is, its meaning is not predictable from the meaning of its parts (cf. Conklin 1962). This criterion eliminates examples (e) – (h) and perhaps also (d).

(ii) Its signification is not included in that of any other color term. This criterion eliminates examples (a) and (b), which are both kinds of red for most speakers of English.

(iii) Its application must not be restricted to a narrow class of objects. This criterion eliminates example (c) which may be predicated only of hair, complexion, and furniture.

(iv) It must be psychologically salient for informants. Indices of psychological salience include, among others, (1) a tendency to occur at the beginning of elicited lists of color terms, (2) stability of reference across informants and across occasions of use, and (3) occurrence in the ideolects of all informants. This criterion eliminates all the examples (a) – (h), most particularly (h).

These criteria (i–iv) suffice in nearly all cases to determine the basic color terms in a given language. The few doubtful cases that arise are handled by the following subsidiary criteria:

(v) The doubtful form should have the same distributional potential as the previously established basic terms. For example, in English, allowing the suffix *-ish,* for example, *reddish, whitish,* and *greenish* are English words, but **aguaish* and **chartreus (e) ish* are not.

(vi) Color terms that are also the name of an object characteristically having that color are suspect, for example, *gold, silver,* and *ash.* This subsidiary criterion would exclude *orange,* in English, *if* it were a doubtful case on the basic criteria (i–iv).

(vii) Recent foreign loan words may be suspect.

(viii) In cases where lexemic status is difficult to assess [see criterion (1)], morphological complexity is given some weight as a secondary criterion. The English term *blue-green* might be eliminated by this criterion.

§ *1.3 Mapping basic color terms*

No informant was asked to map his color terms until the investigator had elicited verbally his full list of basic color terms. Then the stimulus board was covered with an acetate overlay and the informant was given a black grease pencil and asked to indicate for each basic color term, *x:*

(1) all those chips which he would under any conditions call *x*.

(2) the best, most typical examples of *x*.

Each informant was asked to perform the mapping procedure at least three times, at one-week intervals.

Our queries were designed to discover the total area of a basic category and to determine, as well, its focus or most typical members. Often we had access to only one informant for a language. However, in the case of Tzeltal, a Mayan language of southern Mexico, we were able to consult forty informants.

The languages studied were genetically diverse. The choice of each, however, was limited by the availability of informants. All informants were native speakers of their respective languages and, with the exception of the Tzeltal individuals, resided in the San Francisco Bay Area. The primary data include basic color terminologies for the following languages: Arabic (Lebanon), Bulgarian (Bulgaria), Catalan (Spain), Cantonese (China), Mandarin (China), English (United States), Hebrew (Israel), Hungarian (Hungary), Ibibio (Nigeria), Indonesian (Indonesia), Japanese (Japan), Korean (Korea), Pomo (California), Spanish (Mexico), Swahili (East Africa), Tagalog (Philippines), Thai (Thailand), Tzeltal (Southern Mexico), Urdu (India), and Vietnamese (Vietnam).

§ *1.4 Universality of basic color terms*

After all languages were mapped, we made a composite of the foci of all the basic color terms for all the languages. The composite is given in Figure 2; letters indicate the twenty languages

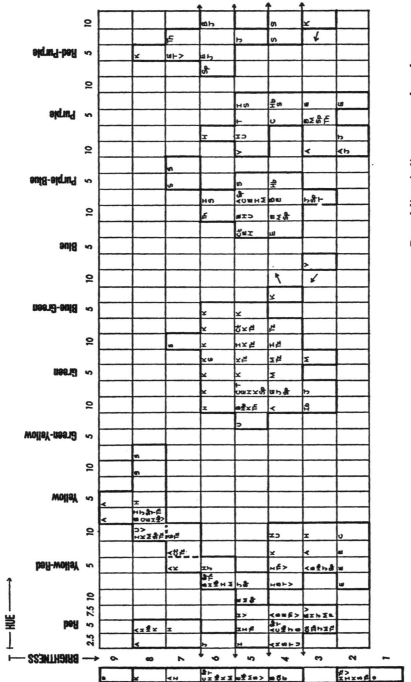

FIGURE 2. COMPOSITE OF FOCI OF BASIC COLOR TERMS IN TWENTY LANGUAGES. NOTE: Dotted lines indicate an overlap of orange and yellow focal areas. These chips represent yellow for Tzeltal and Cantonese, and orange for Arabic and Swahili. * indicates chips chosen as category foci for all twenty languages. Arrows indicate affiliations of categories for the languages indicated. Where a letter occurs more than once on adjacent chips, each was judged a good representative of the focus of the category.

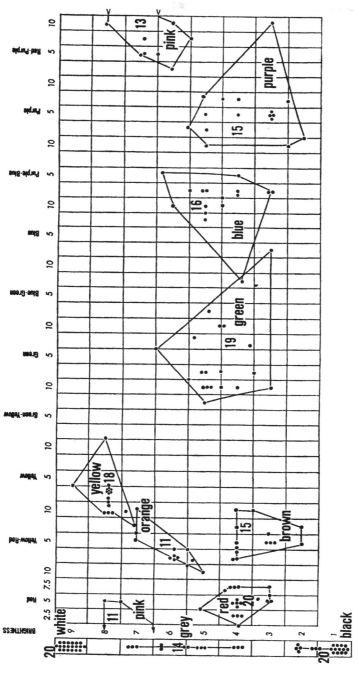

FIGURE 3. NORMALIZED FOCI OF BASIC COLOR TERMS IN TWENTY LANGUAGES. NOTE: Numerals appearing along the borders of the chart refer to the Munsell system of color notation. Numerals appearing on the body of the chart refer to the number of languages in the sample of twenty which encode the corresponding color category. The smallest possible number of lines are used to enclose each color area.

for which we have experimentally collected data. Where several neighboring chips are marked by the same letter, each was judged to be an equally good representative of the focus of a category. Figure 2, although a brute summary of the data and consequently hard to read, nevertheless shows the considerable extent to which the foci of color categories are similar among totally unrelated languages. Both the large blank areas (over 70 per cent of the surface of the chart) and the close clustering of the foci of the various languages into discrete, contiguous areas attest to the failure of the strict linguistic relativity hypothesis. The individual terms and the mapping for each of the twenty languages are given in Appendix I.

The failure of the traditional hypothesis can be seen more clearly in Figure 3. As shown in Figure 2, our informants frequently designated more than one chip as the focus of a color term. Figure 3 is based on a calculation of the center of gravity of the focus area for each basic color term in each language. In each of the eleven areas the number of languages for which the foci are included is indicated by a numeral, and an associated gloss (for example, 'white', 'red') is given. The results shown in Figure 3 support our initial hypothesis: *color categorization is not random and the foci of basic color terms are similar in all languages.*

§ *1.5 Inter-language versus inter-informant variability*

Further evidence for the cross-language universality of color foci is that the location of color foci varies no more between speakers of different languages than between speakers of the same language. In fact, in our tests, speakers of the same language show slightly more variability among themselves than speakers of different languages do. The hypothesis of significant difference *between* languages must consequently be rejected regardless of sampling assumptions, although the small absolute difference in the opposite direction is doubtless insignificant.

The only language for which we have reliable data for a substantial number of informants is Tzeltal; Berlin gathered data from forty Tzeltal informants. Of these, thirty-one located the center of *yaš* in the green area and nine in the blue area; this fact is discussed in detail in § 2.3.4. Tzeltal has five basic color terms: 'white', 'black', 'red', 'green' (that is, *yaš*), and 'yellow'. For the purpose of intralanguage comparison, a random sample of ten informants was selected from among the thirty-one *yaš*-normals.[5]

There are no other languages in our basic sample containing just five terms. However, three languages, Japanese, Korean, and Cantonese, can be reconstructed to five-term systems on the basis of internal evidence (see § 2.4 for detailed discussion of internal linguistic reconstruction of basic color terms). The data for Cantonese, Korean, and Japanese were obtained from a single informant for each language. The foci for 'white', 'black', 'red', 'green', and 'yellow' in these three languages and in Tzeltal were used for the inter-language comparisons.[6]

In order to introduce a finer co-ordinate system for computing inter-focus distances, each unit of hue and each unit of brightness was subdivided into four units, yielding 160 units of hue and thirty-two of brightness. That is, each box in Figure 1 is considered a square of 4-unit side rather than 1-unit side. Each of the ten Tzeltal informants was compared to every other informant, yielding forty-five pairs. For each of the forty-five pairs, the straight-line distance between their foci for each of the five color categories was calculated, resulting in 225 distances (45 informant-pairs × 5 color categories). The overall mean of these 225 inter-informant, intra-language, differences is 4.47 units on the fine scale, or roughly one and one-eighth chip widths.

Then the distances between foci were calculated for each pair of languages for each of the five categories. Two sets of foci were used for Tzeltal in these comparisons: (1) the five foci of a single informant selected at random from the sample of ten, and (2) the five mean foci for the ten informants. The different methods of treating Tzeltal did not affect the result.

Finally, for each pair of languages, the distances for each of the five foci were averaged to determine a single mean distance for every combination of two languages. The results of these

TABLE II

COMPARISON OF MEAN DISTANCES IN THE LOCATION OF FIVE COLOR
FOCI AMONG FOUR LANGUAGES AND AMONG TEN SPEAKERS OF
ONE LANGUAGE

I	Mean inter-focus difference for ten Tzeltal ($ya\acute{s}$-normal) informants	4.47
II	Mean inter-focus difference for all pairs of four languages	
	1. Japanese-Cantonese	4.43
	2. Japanese-Korean	4.30
	3. Cantonese-Korean	4.18
	4. Japanese-Tzeltal	
	(i) one Tzeltal informant	3.84
	[(ii) mean focus for ten Tzeltal informants	3.00]
	5. Cantonese-Tzeltal	
	(i) one Tzeltal informant	2.74
	[(ii) mean focus for ten Tzeltal informants	3.72]
	6. Korean-Tzeltal	
	(i) one Tzeltal informant	2.30
	[(ii) mean focus for ten Tzeltal informants	3.18]

NOTE: The mean absolute inter-informant (intra-language) distance exceeds each absolute inter-language difference. We must consequently reject any hypothesis of significantly greater inter-language than intra-language difference in favor of a null hypothesis of no such difference. In short, controlling for the number of terms, two informants speaking the same language are, on the average, no more similar than two informants speaking different languages.

computations are summarized in Table II, which shows that every inter-language distance is exceeded by the mean inter-informant distance for the sample of Tzeltal informants.

These results controvert the traditional relativistic hypothesis concerning the nature of human color categorization. While it can be argued that bilingualism in English affects the results to some extent (cf. Ervin, 1961), we find it hard to believe that English could so consistently influence the placement of the foci in these diverse languages. Moreover, the work completed with forty Tzeltal informants, who varied from Tzeltal monolinguals to Tzeltal-Spanish bilinguals, indicates that our results are not skewed as a result of bilingualism. Finally, the fact that inter-individual differences in a given language are as great as inter-language differences considerably weakens the possible objection that the bilingualism of the informants consulted distorted our findings.

§ *1.6 Category foci versus category boundaries*

Repeated mapping trials with the same informant and also across informants showed that category foci placements are highly reliable. It is rare that a category focus is displaced by more than two adjacent chips. Category boundaries, however, are not reliable, even for repeated trials with the same inform-ant. This is reflected in the ease with which informants desig-nated foci, in contrast with their difficulty in placing bounda-ries. Subjects hesitated for long periods before performing the latter task, demanded clarification of the instructions, and oth-erwise indicated that this task is more difficult than assigning foci. In fact, in marked contrast to the foci, category bounda-ries proved to be so unreliable, even for an individual inform-ant, that they have been accorded a relatively minor place in the analysis. Consequently, whenever we speak of color cate-gories, *we refer to the foci of categories, rather than to their boundaries or total area,* except when specifically stating other-wise.

Two alternative interpretations of this result suggest them-selves. First, it is possible that the brain's primary storage pro-cedure for the physical reference of color categories is con-cerned with points (or very small volumes) of the color solid rather than extended volumes. Secondary processes, of lower salience and intersubjective homogeneity, would then account for the extensions of reference to points in the color solid not equivalent to (or included in) the focus. Current formal theo-ries of lexical definition are not able to deal naturally with such phenomena. If empirical results of this kind accumulate, simple Boolean function theories of lexical definition will have to be revised in favor of more powerful formalisms.[7] We do not pursue this matter here, especially since there is reason to suspect that color, and perhaps a few other semantic domains such as smell, taste, and noise, have unusual lexical properties.

The alternative explanation is that this is a peculiarity of our experimental procedure. In retrospect, we find nothing which would be likely to produce such a bias. Moreover, the evolutionary scheme, including the data from the additional languages ordered by it, works so well in terms of foci that it argues against interpreting the apparent reality of foci as an artifact of the method.

§ 2 EVOLUTION OF BASIC COLOR TERMS

Our second major conclusion is that there appears to be a fixed sequence of evolutionary stages through which a language must pass as its basic color vocabulary increases.

This conclusion is based in part on the substantiation of the universality of the eleven basic category foci, in part on the non-randomness of their distribution across contemporary languages (and certain logical consequences of the particular distribution found), and in part on additional data and arguments to be introduced below.

An important methodological consequence of the universality finding is that we have been able to expand our data base from the twenty languages treated experimentally to a larger number, reported with varying degrees of precision in the general literature. Once the basic universal category foci are established, meaningful comparison can often be made with literary accounts of color nomenclatures.[8] It may be that the traditional relativistic position has derived in part from a confusion of noncomparability of *descriptions* of systems with random variation of structure among the systems themselves.

As shown in rule (1), the basic color categories are partially ordered in six equivalence classes, so that if a language encodes a category from a given class, it must encode all categories from each prior class. This empirical generalization holds, not only for the original twenty languages investigated, but for all languages in our sample (with the minor exceptions discussed in § 2.5). There is no reason to suppose that this generalization, which applies so clearly in the present, should not apply also in the past; at least, we know of no result from historical linguistics—or any other discipline—which would impel such an otherwise unmotivated complication of assumptions. Accepting then, that rule (1) applies also to prior stages of individual languages, it follows that for a language to gain or lose color terms it must do so in the order specified by rule (1). Although it is logically as possible for languages to lose basic color terms as to gain them over time, this appears rarely, if ever, to actually happen. In our consideration of ninety-eight languages, which involved the assessment of comparative and internal historical evidence, we have so far found no indication of the loss of a basic color term.[9]

Hence, the six equivalence classes of rule (1) may be interpreted as representing at least six evolutionary stages of complexity of basic color lexicon, which have the following properties: that a given language at a given point of time can be assigned to one and only one stage; and that a language currently in a given stage must historically have passed through all prior stages in the appropriate order.

We say "at least" six evolutionary stages because, in fact, the data lead us to posit seven stages. In particular, as suggested in the discussion of rule (1) in § 1, the emergence of green and yellow each signals a separate stage of development, despite the fact that yellow occasionally appears before green. That is, we consider Stage III to be signalled by the appearance of either green or yellow and Stage IV to be signalled by the appearance of whichever of the two did not appear at Stage III.

Our data contain too many four-term systems to allow us to postulate the simultaneous occurrence of the fourth and fifth terms. If we contrast the first and last equivalence classes of rule (1), we find a different situation. In the case of {black, white}, we find no instance of a language possessing one term and not the other; that is, there are no one-term systems. Similarly, for {purple, pink, orange, grey}, there is a strong tendency for a language which possesses one of these terms to possess all of them. Of the twenty Stage VII systems we have found, nine or 45 per cent, contain all eleven terms, hence all members of the class {purple, pink, orange, grey}. Furthermore, the list of eleven-term systems could be expanded considerably by adding all the Indo-European languages of Europe, bringing the above noted proportion to at least 70 per cent. On the other hand, while our data show eighteen Stage IV systems (those containing terms for both green and yellow), they also show seventeen systems with terms for either green or yellow but not both.

These facts argue against the simultaneous appearance of green and yellow.

§ *2.1 Basic color lexicon and technological/cultural complexity*

In addition to the fact that the stages of complexity of color vocabulary have a temporal ordering, there appears to be a positive correlation between general cultural complexity (and/or level of technological development) and complexity of color vocabulary. All the languages of highly industrialized European and Asian peoples are Stage VII, while all representatives of early Stages (I, II, and III) are spoken by peoples with small populations and limited technology, located in isolated areas. However, this kind of correlation cannot be established with precision until concepts such as "level of technological development" and "degree of cultural complexity" are better understood and more precisely measured than they are at present. Such information as we have, although vague, suggests that the sequence of elaboration of color lexicon is an evolutionary one accompanying, and perhaps a reflex of, increasing technological and cultural advancement.

The total vocabularies of languages spoken by peoples possessing relatively simple technologies tend to be smaller than those of highly complex civilizations. Moreover, it seems likely that the earliest languages spoken by man had extremely small vocabularies, perhaps not many times greater than the repertoires of discreet verbal signs used by apes and monkeys.[10] Thus, increase in the number of basic color terms may be seen as part of a general increase in vocabulary, a response to an informationally richer cultural environment about which speakers must communicate effectively. There is also some evidence to suggest that for groups living "close to nature," basic color terms are of relatively little adaptive value because of their broadness of reference (Post, 1962). For example, to a group whose members have frequent occasion to contrast fine shades of leaf color and who possess no dyed fabrics, color-coded electrical wires, and so forth, it may not be worthwhile to rote-learn labels for gross perceptual discriminations such as green/ blue, despite the psychophysical salience of such contrasts.[11]

The above argument is not offered as conclusive but as a

plausible speculation about the cultural evolutionary mechanisms which account for the growth in size of basic color lexicon. In any case, the argument is addressed only to the problem of increase in size of color vocabulary and does not attempt to explain the particular order in which color foci universally become encoded in individual lexicons. The latter topic is a difficult problem which is only vaguely understood at this time. We will return briefly to this point in § 4.

§ 2.2 *The seven stages in the evolution of basic color terms*

Stage I in the evolution of lexical color categories is represented by just two terms: *black* plus most dark hues, and *white* plus most light hues. For convenience we will write these categories BLACK and WHITE. Stage I is represented in Figure 4.[12]

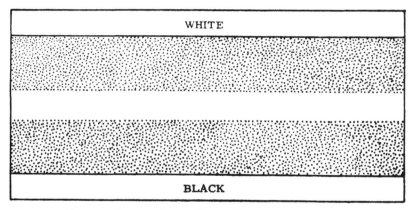

FIGURE 4. TYPICAL STAGE I BASIC COLOR LEXICON

At Stage II a third category emerges which we call RED. RED includes all reds, oranges, most yellows, browns, pinks, and purples (including violet). WHITE and BLACK continue to segment the middle-range hues. Stage II is represented in Figure 5.

At Stage III the reduction in scope of WHITE and BLACK continues and a new category emerges. This may be either GREEN or YELLOW. GREEN normally includes English yellow-green, greens, blue-greens, blues, and blue-purples; it may, however, include only greens plus yellow-greens and tans or light browns (as in Hanunóo, § 2.3.3). We designate the addi-

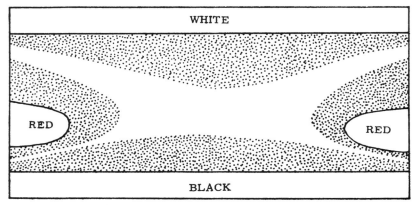

FIGURE 5. TYPICAL STAGE II BASIC COLOR LEXICON

tion of the GREEN category at Stage III as Stage IIIa. If the
YELLOW category is added at Stage III the extension is always
into light greens and light browns or tans. This development
is designated Stage IIIb. Stages IIIa and IIIb are depicted in
figures 6A and 6B respectively.

At Stage IV YELLOW or GREEN, whichever did not emerge at
the previous stage, now emerges. The GREEN term now includes
most blues, irrespective of the variant of Stage III through
which the language has passed. RED continues to encompass the
areas of English red, some yellow-reds, purple, and purple-reds.

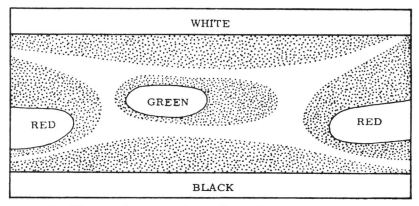

FIGURE 6A. TYPICAL STAGE IIIa BASIC COLOR LEXICON

GREEN *extended into blues. In Hanunóo,* GREEN *includes greens, yellow
greens, tans & browns.*

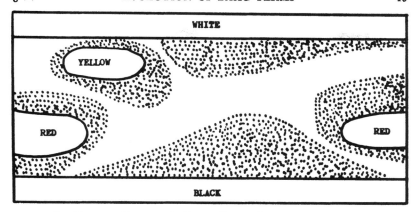

FIGURE 6B. TYPICAL STAGE IIIb BASIC COLOR LEXICON

YELLOW *extended into greens*

Presumably, BLACK and WHITE continue to be deprived of hue reference, becoming increasingly restricted to neutral values. Stage IV is shown in Figure 7.

At Stage V the focus of blue emerges from the GREEN area. GREEN now becomes green. At this stage, BLACK and WHITE are fully reduced to black and white, that is, to neutral values. The RED area is probably also reduced, losing purples and violets. Stage V is depicted in Figure 8.

Stage VI, the last at which a single focus appears, introduces brown. At Stage VI both RED and YELLOW become even more

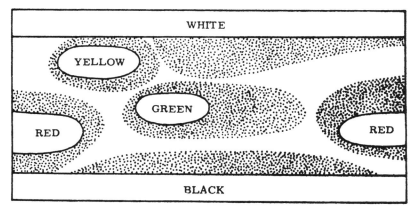

FIGURE 7. TYPICAL STAGE IV BASIC COLOR LEXICON

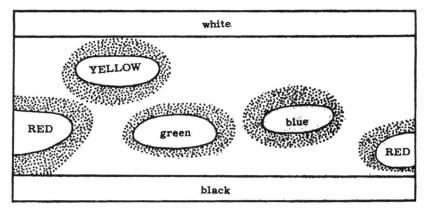

FIGURE 8. TYPICAL STAGE V BASIC COLOR LEXICON

restricted in scope although it is not until Stage VII that they become red and yellow. Stage VI is seen in Figure 9.

When the color lexicon expands beyond seven terms, that is, beyond Stage VI, there is a rapid expansion to the full roster of eleven basic color categories. This conclusion is suggested by the fact that, for the ninety-eight languages investigated, only eleven color lexicons belong to types other than 1, 2, 3, 4, 5, 6, 7 and 22 (see Table III). Apparently, at Stage VII, the remaining basic categories, purple, pink, orange, and grey, are quickly added to the lexicon and, as far as we have been

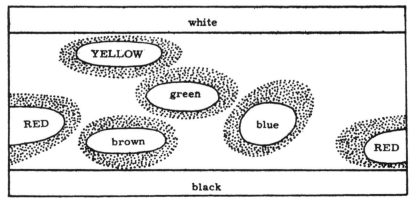

FIGURE 9. TYPICAL STAGE VI BASIC COLOR LEXICON

TABLE III

DISTRIBUTION OF NINETY-EIGHT BASIC COLOR LEXICONS AMONG THE TWENTY-TWO THEORETICALLY POSSIBLE TYPES, WITH INDICATION OF EVOLUTIONARY STAGE

Type	No. of Basic Color Terms	Stage	No. of Examples	
1	2	I	9	9
2	3	II	21	21
3	4	IIIa	8	
4	4	IIIb	9	17
5	5	IV	18 ª	18
6	6	V	8 ᵇ	8
7	7	VI	5	5
8	8	VII	1	
9	8	VII	0	
10	8	VII	0	
11	8	VII	1	
12	9	VII	0	
13	9	VII	0	
14	9	VII	1	
15	9	VII	0	
16	9	VII	1 ᶜ	
17	9	VII	0	
18	10	VII	1	
19	10	VII	3 ᵈ	
20	10	VII	3	
21	10	VII	0	
22	11	VII	9 ᵉ	20
			Total 98	98

KEY TO TABLE III. a. Western Apache, Hopi and Papago are Stage IV systems, but have six terms. See §§ 2.5 and 3.4.
b. Samal is a Stage V system, but may have seven terms. See §§ 2.5 and 3.5.
c. Cantonese has only eight terms. See §§ 2.5 and 3.7.
d. Vietnamese has only nine terms. See §§ 2.5 and 3.7.
e. Hungarian and Russian have twelve terms each. See §§ 2.3.7 and 3.7.

able to ascertain, in no particular order. Our data suggest that purple and pink probably arise from RED although occasionally purple may come from BLACK. Orange usually becomes isolated from YELLOW but there is some evidence to indicate that in some cases it may have arisen from RED. Grey represents simply the encoding of mid-brightness neutral hues between black and white.

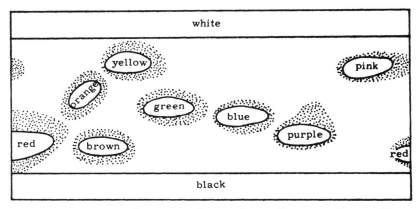

FIGURE 10. TYPICAL STAGE VII BASIC COLOR LEXICON, ELEVEN-TERM SYSTEM *

Stage VII systems include all eight-, nine-, ten-, and eleven-term systems; they thus include types 8–22. As shown in Table III, of the twenty Stage VII systems so far encountered, nine are of type 22, that is, they contain all eleven basic categories, while seven of the fifteen possible types of Stage VII are not represented at all (cf. note 5, also § 2.3). An eleven-term Stage VII system is seen in Figure 10.

To summarize to this point, at least seven stages may be recognized in the evolution of basic color terms. These stages and their basic color terms are as follows:

Stage I BLACK, WHITE (two terms)
Stage II BLACK, WHITE, RED (three terms)

* The eleventh category, grey, cannot be depicted on the above diagram given the conventions discussed in Note 12.

Stage IIIa BLACK, WHITE, RED, GREEN (extending into blues) (four terms)
Stage IIIb BLACK, WHITE, RED, YELLOW (four terms)
  Stage IV BLACK, WHITE, RED, GREEN, YELLOW (five terms)
   Stage V black, white, RED, green, YELLOW, blue (six terms)
  Stage VI black, white, RED, green, YELLOW, blue, brown (seven terms)
Stage VII black, white, red, green, yellow, blue, brown, purple, pink, orange, grey (eight, nine, ten, or eleven terms)

§ 2.3 Some typical systems

Our search of the literature for reports on color terminologies is admittedly incomplete. Nonetheless, we have gathered reasonably reliable information on seventy-eight languages in addition to the twenty languages for which we have experimental data. The results from all reliably reported languages are considered in §§ 3.1–3.7. They conform almost totally to our proposed evolutionary sequence. In the following subsections (2.3.1–2.3.7) we give several examples of each stage, with emphasis on the earlier, more interesting stages.

§ 2.3.1 Stage I systems [BLACK, WHITE]

Originally, we did not expect to discover an extant example of Stage I. We were thus pleasantly surprised to receive from K.-F. Koch the following report on the Jalé, a New Guinea Highland group, whose language has tentatively been classified as Danian (non-Austronesian). In a report made in our seminar, Koch, who was unaware of our findings, stoutly resisted suggestions that Jalé might have more than two true color terms. Jalé is Stage I, having basic color terms only for 'BLACK' and 'WHITE' (see Figure 11). There are other terms which, in highly specialized contexts, refer to certain hues; however, these terms are restricted almost exclusively to particular substances or objects, for example, mut 'red soil', and pianó 'name of plant whose leaves are used to rub yarn, dying it a green color'. Koch reports that when he referred to a 'green' object with pianó, he was consistently misunderstood. He subse-

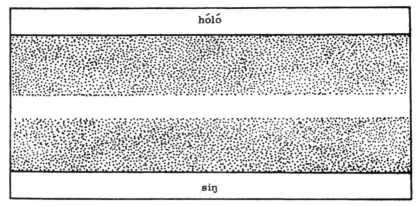

FIGURE 11. INFERRED COLOR CATEGORIES FOR JALÉ, REPRESENTING STAGE I

quently learned to use the term *siŋ* 'BLACK' or *hóló* 'WHITE',
depending on the degree of brightness the particular green
represented. That Jalé is in fact a Stage I system was made even
more obvious when he reported that the appearance of blood
is *siŋ* 'BLACK', exactly as 'blood (red)' should be at Stage I because of its low brightness.

Additional evidence of Stage I systems in Highland New
Guinea has recently been presented by Bromley (1967), who
also worked with Danian languages of the Grand Valley. Of
the seven tribal groups for which Bromley published the native
forms, three may be interpreted as exhibiting Stage I color
terminology. Three of the remaining languages are probably
Stage II systems, that is, they have added a term for RED, and
one language is ambiguous in classification.

Bromley's comments on the problems presented by the basic
color vocabulary of these groups are of particular interest. "In
much of the area under study there are overlapping color taxonomies, one dividing all colors into two categories, 'brilliant',
including most reds, yellow and white, and 'dull', including
most greens and black. In various parts of the area 'white' and
'red' are also labelled by other simple terms, and an informant
may either respond with one of the two general terms or one
of the narrower special terms [that is, secondary terms]. Widely
varying descriptive phrases are used for other specific color

terms; recurring examples are 'fresh leaf' for 'green' and 'cut orchid-fibres' for 'yellow'. . . . It would appear that [of] the languages under study several . . . lack basic color terms other than 'brilliant' and 'dull'." (1967:288).

Those languages of the Highland New Guinea area which show Stage I terminology are the Upper Pyramid group, the Pyramid-Wodo groups and the Hitigima group of the Lower Valley. Upper Pyramid terms are *muli* 'black, green' and *mola* 'white, red, yellow'. Pyramid-Wodo terms are *muδi* 'black' and *moδa* 'white, red, yellow'. A descriptive term *getega* is cited for 'green', but is analyzed as a compound of the words for 'fresh' *get* and 'leaf' *ega*. Finally, the Tangma group of the Lower Valley (Lower Valley Hitigima) shows a simple two-term system with *muli* covering black and green and *mola* referring to white, red, yellow. (See Bromley 1967:305–306 for the 100-word Swadesh lists for these groups.) That we should find Stage I systems in Highland New Guinea is consonant with the association of simple color lexicon with simple technological and cultural development.

§ 2.3.2 *Stage II systems* [introduction of RED]

Stage II systems are found in several areas of the world, especially Melanesia, Australia, Africa, and parts of the New World. A typical example of such systems can be seen in Tiv, a Bantoid language of Nigeria. Paul Bohannan notes: "In Tiv . . . all green, some blues, and some greys are *ii*. But very light blues and light greys are *pupu*. *Nyian*, which covers brown, also covers all warm colors through red to yellow. The distinction between *ii* and *pupu* actually is not in terms of color, but in terms of what we would call shade—darkness and lightness. Very light blue, grey, or white are all *pupu*. *Ii* means dark and covers all dark colors and black—unless there is a warm color present; brown, red and yellow are all *nyian*. Tiv can distinguish colors and do color-blind tests, but their culture does not require—or allow—that they make some of the color distinctions that Westerners make. Westerners are the most color-conscious of peoples" (1963:35–36). A schematic representation of Tiv is seen in Figure 12.

A second African language exhibiting Stage II basic color

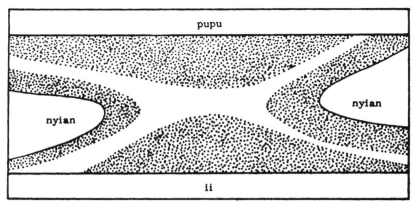

FIGURE 12. INFERRED COLOR CATEGORIES FOR TIV, REPRESENTING STAGE II

terminology is described by Turner (1966) for the Ndembu, a Benue-Congo speaking people of the Congo. Discussing in detail the ritual significance of color, Turner states: "This tripartite classification relates to the colours white [*tooka*], red [*ku-chinana*] and black [*wuyila*]. These are the only colours for which Ndembu possess primary terms. Terms for other colours are either derivates from these—as in the case of *chi-tookoloka* 'grey', which is derived from *tooka*, 'white'—or consist of descriptive and metaphorical phrases, as in the case of 'green', *meji amatamba,* which means 'water of sweet potato leaves'. Very frequently, colours which we would distinguish from white, red, and black are, by Ndembu, linguistically identified with them. Blue cloth, for example, is described as 'black' cloth, and yellow or orange objects are lumped together as 'red'. Sometimes a yellow object may be described as '*neyi nsela*', 'like beeswax', but yellow is often regarded as ritually equivalent to red" (Turner 1966:47–48) .

The Nasioi of Bougainville are another example of Stage II if the term for 'red' is indeed a basic term and not simply descriptive. (In the latter case the system would exemplify Stage I.) Eugene Ogan, in a personal communication, reports: "I worked a total of twenty-six months among Nasioi speakers. The only words I heard in regular use which might be described as 'color terms' were *kakara* 'white', mutaŋa 'black, dark' and erereŋ 'red'. The etymology of the last word is clear: ereŋ

'blood'. I know of no such etymology for the other two words."
Nasioi is a non-Austronesian language.

An example similar to the Nasioi, where the term for red is
also the word for blood, comes from Rivers' research on the
aborigines of the Seven Rivers District, Queensland, Australia.
"Most of these natives . . . seemed to agree in having only three
definite words in their colour vocabulary, *viz.*, ŏti or owang for
red and colours containing red, yŏpa or wăpŏk for white and
light colours, and unma, or manara, for black and dark colours.
Manara was the word used for the colour of the skin [and] . . .
ŏti is said to be the word for blood" (Rivers 1901a:88).

Our arguments for the maximum extension of RED at Stage II
to include not only high brightness hues such as 'yellow',
'orange', and 'pink', but 'brown' and 'violet' as well are given
support by Rivers' summary of the literature.

"The absence of a word for brown appears to be characteristic of very many languages, probably of the great majority of
the languages of the world. Among those which I have had an
opportunity of investigating, I have found no word for brown
in several Australian, Melanesian, and Polynesian languages, in
Tamil, Eskimo, Welsh and the Arabic of the Egyptian peasant.
The absence of a word for brown has been noted in many other
races. Bastian notes that the Siamese call brown 'dam-deng'
meaning 'black-red'. Kotelmann found that the Lapps called
brown 'tscharpis roksad' again meaning 'black-red'. The Ainus
call brown 'furiambe', red being fure. Pergens found that of
the fifty-seven Congolese examined by him, only two could give
a word for brown; one called it moindo, which was also used
for black, and the other 'ossingaiumbayéta', m'bayéta being
used for pink. Gatschet records that a word for brown is absent
from several American Indian (Amerind) languages, while in
others there may be several terms for this colour. It is possible
that, in the latter case, the words used were names for special
browns, as in Mabuiag, and were not true generic terms for
brown . . .

"Schellong gives 'mela' as a word for brown in two Melanesian languages. This is probably the same word as 'mera',
which is a common Melanesian term for 'red'.

"There appears to have been no word in Homeric Greek

which one can regard as equivalent to brown, and I am indebted to a note from the Rev. H. T. F. Duckworth that the same is true of the Greek spoken by the majority of the inhabitants of Cyprus at the present day. They call dark brown objects μαυροσ which is the word in common use for black, while other brown objects are called κόκκινόζ, which is also applied to brilliant scarlet" (Rivers 1901a:68–69).

§ *2.3.3 Stage III systems* [introduction of GREEN or YELLOW]

Stage III terminologies have been reported from several parts of the world. On the basis of our search of the literature to date, a large number are found in Africa, certain areas of Malaya and the Philippines, and Australia. We use Ibibio, a Nigerian language, as the exemplary case of Stage IIIa, as Elaine Kaufman (n.d.) gathered the data using our experimental method. Ibibio has basic color terms glossed 'WHITE', 'BLACK', 'RED', and 'GREEN', which are displayed in Figure 13A.

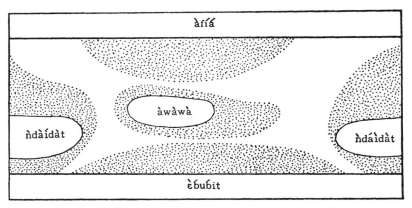

FIGURE 13A. INFERRED COLOR CATEGORIES FOR IBIBIO, REPRESENTING STAGE IIIa

Hanunóo, a Philippine language of Mindoro, represents Stage IIIa, but is somewhat variant in the extension of GREEN. The term for 'BLACK' in Hanunóo, *(ma) biru,* ranges over black, violet, indigo, blue, dark green, dark grey and deep shades of other colors and mixtures; 'WHITE' *(ma) lagti?* includes white and light tints of other colors and mixtures; 'RED' *(ma) rara?* includes maroon, red, orange, yellow, and mixtures in which these qualities are seen to predominate; 'GREEN' (ma) latuy covers light green and mixtures of green, yellow and light brown (see Conklin, 1955). That (ma) latuy is best considered a IIIa variant, rather than IIIb, is evidenced by Conklin's gloss of the term as "relative presence of light greenness; greenness" (1955:190). The inferred distribution of Hanunóo color terms can be seen in Figure 13B.

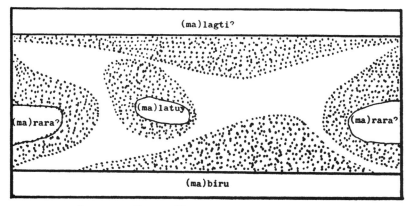

FIGURE 13B. INFERRED COLOR CATEGORIES FOR HANUNÓO, REPRESENTING A VARIANT OF STAGE IIIa

Rivers (1901a) reports two groups exhibiting Stage IIIa color vocabularies. One is found on Tanna Island in the Torres Straits, off the southeastern New Guinea coast. Another tribe is found along the Fitzroy River in Queensland. For the Tanna Island group, Rivers notes the terms *ratuan* 'white', *rapen* 'black', *laulau* 'red', and *ramimera* 'green.' There also exist several terms which appear to be simple modifications of the above basic forms. Thus 'brown' is *rapenmeruk ~ rapenakin < rapen* 'black'; 'purple' is *laulauakin < laulau* 'red'; 'orange' and 'yellow' are also derived from 'red', being termed *lauiha* and *lauihameruk*, respectively; 'blue' *ramimeraakin*, 'indigo' *ramimera-ramimera*, and 'violet' *ramimerabuk* all appear as derivations of *ramimera* 'green.' Rivers notes this feature when he describes the "free use of qualifying suffixes, red, purple, orange, and yellow being all named by some modification of one word [red] while green, blue, and violet were named by some modification of another [green]" (Rivers, 1901a:85).

There are a number of examples of Stage IIIb systems, that is, where YELLOW has emerged while green and blue hues continue to be included in BLACK (and to a lesser extent, WHITE) or designated by descriptives.

Ibo, a language of Nigeria, exhibits this variant of Stage III terminology. There are basic terms for 'BLACK' *ojĭ*, 'WHITE' *nzu*, 'RED' *uhie*, and 'YELLOW' *odo*. The word utilized for green hues is a secondary (non-basic) color term *agwokwondu* meaning roughly 'it has the color of leaves' (Goldberg, n.d.). The Ibo distribution is seen in Figure 13c.

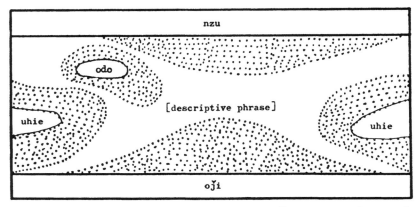

FIGURE 13C. INFERRED COLOR CATEGORIES FOR IBO REPRESENTING STAGE IIIb

Urhobo is also a IIIb system, with recent loan words for the indigenously unnamed green-blue area. Thus, we see terms for 'BLACK' *ɔbyibi*, 'WHITE' *ɔfuafu*, 'RED' *ɔBaBare*, and 'YELLOW' *ɔdo*. The English loans *grini* and *blu* refer to 'green' and 'blue' respectively and are best not treated as basic forms (*Ibid.*).

The Fitzroy River aborigines studied by Rivers (1901a) have four terms, *bura* 'white', *guru* 'black, blue, indigo', *kiran* 'red, purple', and *kalmur* 'yellow, green, orange, blue-green'. This is another example of a Stage IIIb system. In comparison with a simple Stage II system described for the Queensland group mentioned earlier, he notes: "in addition to definite words for red, white and black, the Fitzroy natives had a name 'kalmur' which they used for yellows and greens" (1901a:89). He summarizes his work on this group by noting that "there can be no doubt as to the main features of the colour terminology of these tribes. In all cases there were definite words for black, white, and red, the word for red being used also for purple and in some cases for orange. The Fitzroy natives seemed to differ from those of the Seven Rivers in that a fairly definite name for yellow and green [as a unitary category] had also been evolved. Blue and violet were by nearly all given the same name as black. There appeared to be no trace of a word for brown" (*ibid*:89).

§ *2.3.4 Stage IV systems* [introduction of YELLOW or GREEN]

Stage IV terminologies are represented in many languages of the world. Our data show them to occur in large numbers in the New World and Africa.

In Central America we find Stage IV systems in many of the aboriginal languages of the area. To our knowledge, all of the twenty-six Mayan languages of Mexico and Guatemala exhibit Stage IV color terminology. We have chosen Tzeltal as the exemplary case of Stage IV as we have collected data from this language utilizing the experimental methods discussed earlier.[13]

Tzeltal has five basic color terms which are *ʔihk'* 'BLACK', *sak* 'WHITE', *cah* 'RED', *yaš* 'GREEN', and *k'an* 'YELLOW'. The distribution of these terms may be seen in Figure 14.

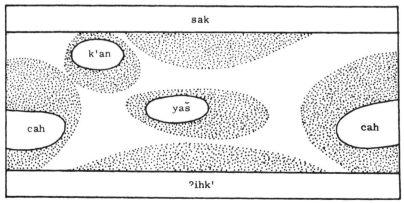

FIGURE 14. INFERRED COLOR CATEGORIES FOR TZELTAL, REPRESENTING STAGE IV

The treatment of the category *yaš* 'GREEN' in Tzeltal is of particular interest because some of the data suggest that this language may now be transitional from Stage IV to Stage V.

Of the forty Tzeltal informants from whom we gathered experimental data, thirty-one indicated that the focal point of *yaš* falls precisely in the area of the spectrum which corresponds to focal English green. In general usage, the maximum extension of *yaš* includes greens, blue-greens, blues and some blue-purples. However, when greater specification of *yaš* is requested, many informants restrict the term almost exclusively to greens and some blue-greens. 'Blues' and 'purple-blues' are recognized as a distinct area and are designated by a descriptive phrase, *ʔihk' ʔihk'tik šyašal* 'blackish green' or simply *ʔihk' ʔihk'-tik* 'blackish'. In at least one instance, an informant referred to this area by the Spanish term *azul* 'blue'.

The remaining nine informants in our sample of forty have essentially the same maximal extension of *yaš* as the previous thirty-one individuals (that is, over greens and blues) but the focal point of the category is in the blue area. When greater specificity is requested for the greens and blue-greens, descriptive phrases are often utilized, for example, *saksaktik šyašal* 'whitish green'.

Perhaps the most likely interpretation for these data is that Tzeltal is moving from Stage IV to V, and the ambiguity of the focus for *yaš* reflects the transition. It is apparent to all Tzeltal speakers that *yaš* includes two major *perceptual* centers, green and blue. In the contact with speakers of Spanish over the last 400 years, this fact has probably been accentuated many times. Speakers of Tzeltal respond by reducing the extension of *yaš* in instances where specificity is required either to greens (for most informants) or to blues (for the minority), treating the remaining area with a descriptive phrase. Tzeltal may continue for many generations to rely on such descriptives to designate what is clearly an incipient lexical category best glossed 'blue'. It is our prediction, however, that as Tzeltal speakers become more exposed to Spanish in the schools, *yaš* will eventually be restricted entirely to greens and that *azul* or some other Spanish term will be adopted for the perceptual category 'blue', rendering Tzeltal a standard Stage V system.

Another New World Stage IV system can be seen in Tarascan, an unclassified language of the state of Michoacan, Mexico. Mary Foster, a linguist who has worked on Tarascan for several years, reports the following terms: *urá-* 'white,' *turí-* 'black,' *čaṛá-* 'red,' *šuná-* 'green,' and *cipá-n-* (*pe*) 'yellow.' Foster indicates that a term 'blue' *ciránki* is "aberrant in that it doesn't occur with the adjectival *-pe* suffix. Gilberti's 16th century dictionary gives *cicípu* for blue. The word *ciránki* also means 'blue ear of corn' " (personal communication).

In Africa, we may cite as illustrative of Stage IV the color terminology of the Daza, a Nilo-Saharan group of Eastern Nigeria. Le Coeur (1956) reports the following terms: *cuo* 'blanc'; *yasko* 'noir'; *maaḍo* 'rouge'; *zẹdẹ* 'vert, bleu' (and perhaps in some cases, 'jaune clair' and 'violet') , and *mini* 'jaune'.

A second African system apparently of this stage is that of the !Kung Bushmen of South Africa. Richard Lee, in a personal communication, reports the following forms: *!gow* 'white, grey'; *žho* 'black'; *!gã* 'red, rust'; */ouŋ* 'green, blue, violet', and *gow* 'yellow, orange, tan'.

§ *2.3.5 Stage V systems* [introduction of blue]

So far, we have found Stage V systems in Africa, southern India, and the Philippines. Mandarin Chinese may also, on further investigation, prove to be a Stage V language.

A typical Stage V color vocabulary is seen in the Plains Tamil of South India. P. M. Gardner (1966a) reports the following terms: *veḷḷai* 'white'; *karuppu* 'black'; *sivappu* 'red'; *paccai* 'green'; *manjal* 'yellow' and *nīlam* 'blue'. The inferred distribution of these terms is seen in Figure 15.

Interpreting the report of Robinson (1925), we have classified Hausa as Stage V with the following forms: *fāri,* 'white', *băḳi* 'black', *ja* 'red', *algashi* 'green', *nawaya* 'yellow,' and *shuḍi* 'blue'.

A second African group exhibiting basic terms for six colors is Nupe, a Niger-Congo language of the Kwa branch located in

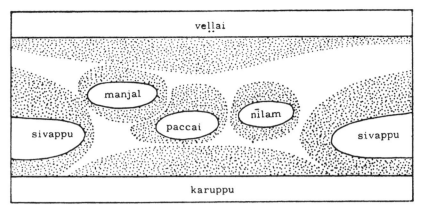

FIGURE 15. INFERRED COLOR CATEGORIES FOR PLAINS TAMIL, REPRESENTING
STAGE V

Nigeria. Banfield and MacIntyre (1915) report *bókùṇ* 'white',
ẓìkò 'black, dark blue', *dzúfú* 'red', *áligà* 'green', *wǫṇjiṇ* 'yellow,' and *dòfa* '(light) blue'.

§ *2.3.6 Stage VI systems* [introduction of brown]

Stage VI systems, although rather sparsely represented in our
sample, are found in southern India, Africa, and North America. The color terminology of Nez Perce, an American Indian
language of the state of Washington, is depicted in Figure 16.

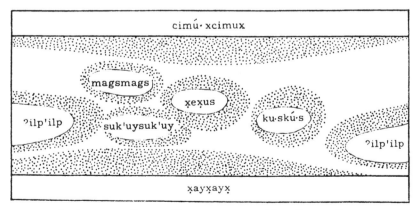

FIGURE 16. INFERRED COLOR CATEGORIES FOR NEZ PERCE, REPRESENTING
STAGE VI

Aoki, who has worked on Nez Perce for several summers, reports, in a personal communication, the following terms:
cimú·xcimux 'white', *xayxayx* 'black', *ʔilp'ilp* 'red', *xexus*
'green', *magsmags* 'yellow', *ku·skú·s* 'blue', and *suk'uysuk'uy*
'brown'.

Stage VI is also seen in some dialects of Malayalam of southern India, for example, *vellá* 'white', *kaḍúpə* 'black', *čuwə́ppə*
'red', *paččá* 'green', *maṇṇá* 'yellow', *niḷá* 'blue', and *tavita*
'brown' (Goodman, 1963:9–10).

We have at least two examples of this stage in Africa, the
Bari and the Siwi. Bari terms are *-kwe* 'white', *-rnö* 'black', *-tor*
'red', *-ngem* 'green', *-forong* 'yellow', *-murye* 'blue', and *-jere*
'brown' (Owen, 1908). Siwi terms are *aztùf* 'white', *amilàl*
'black', *azgahh* 'red', *ówràrr* 'green', *lasfàrr* 'yellow', *asmáwêê*
'blue', and *lasmàrr* 'brown' (Walker 1921).

§ 2.3.7 *Stage VII systems* [eight-, nine-, ten-, and eleven-term systems]

Stage VII is represented by twenty of the ninety-eight languages
in our sample, and varying types of this stage are found widely
in the world's languages. As indicated in § 2.3 and in Table III,
the most frequently occurring Stage VII systems exhibit all
eleven basic color terms, *white, black, red, green, yellow, blue,
brown, purple, pink, orange,* and *grey*. At least two of the languages in our experimental sample, Urdu and Cantonese, possess only eight basic color terms. We may tentatively treat these
languages as early Stage VII systems. Urdu has terms for black,
white, red, green, yellow, blue, brown, and purple, but lacks
terms for orange, pink and grey. Likewise, Cantonese has yet
to add brown, purple or orange to its basic inventory (see § 2.5).
Tagalog lacks a term for orange as does Vietnamese. Finally,
Catalan lacks pink and orange terms.

Hungarian presents a special case. It has basic terms for the
ten basic categories exclusive of red and two basic terms for red.
If this finding is borne out by further research, it may be possible to suggest developmental stages other than those already
mentioned. Similarly, Russian, as well as several other Slavic
languages, is reported to have two basic terms for blue: *siniy*
'dark-blue' and *goluboy* 'light blue'. The status of *goluboy* as

a basic term is, however, not clear. The work of Istomina (1963) shows *goluboy* to be less salient and less well understood by Russian children than the Russian terms for red, green, yellow, dark-blue (*siniy*), orange and purple. Our own interviews with Russian-speaking informants are not conclusive but suggest that, for some speakers at least, *siniy* marks two categories—one includes *goluboy* and one contrasts with *goluboy*. Thus, depending on context, *siniy* has two senses, 'blue' and 'dark-blue', as illustrated in Figure 17. If this formulation is generally correct, *goluboy* must be considered a secondary

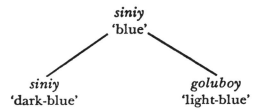

FIGURE 17. SEMANTIC RELATIONSHIPS OF RUSSIAN SINIY AND GOLUBOY

term in Russian. The same argument may perhaps apply to Hungarian *vörös* 'dark red'.

A total summary of the available data relevant to the evolutionary hypothesis from ninety-eight languages is given in § 2.6, where all interpretable reports are summarized and the stage, linguistic classification, basic color terms, and source of data are given for each language listed.

All languages examined confirm the evolutionary hypothesis in every detail except as noted in § 2.5. English, a typical Stage VII, eleven-term system, is depicted in Figure 10.

§ 2.4 Internal linguistic reconstruction of basic color terms

Our arguments concerning the development of basic color categories have been based primarily on the pattern of the distribution of such categories across contemporary languages. The partial ordering we found was seen to be most simply explained in terms of evolutionary assumptions. The evolutionary argument could be further strengthened by two kinds of evidence. The stronger kind would consist in the linguistic reconstruction of color vocabulary for one particular language family, for example, Indo-European. Some early philological work of Gladstone (1858) and Geiger (1880) moved in this direction but their work lacks careful application of the comparative method (see Appendix III). What is clearly needed is a modern reconstruction of Indo-European color terms.

We do, however, have considerable independent evidence of a weaker kind: internal linguistic reconstruction. This method is a common procedure in historical linguistics. The relevance of internal reconstruction for ethnology was best stated by Sapir in his classic *Time Perspective* monograph (1916). The method has been recently employed by Romney (1967) in his reconstruction of Yuman kinship terminology.

In regard to the internal reconstruction of color vocabulary, at least two assumptions of the method are primary:

(1) Color terms that can be shown on linguistic grounds to be loan words are likely to be more recent additions than native color terms.

(2) Color terms that are analyzable are likely to be more recent additions than unanalyzable terms. Analyzability may take five forms:

    (i) color terms containing derivational affixes are more recent additions than color terms not containing derivational affixes;

    (ii) color terms containing more than one stem are more recent additions than those containing a single stem;

    (iii) color terms which contain analyzable stems and/or affixes are more recent additions than those which contain unanalyzable stems and/or affixes;

    (iv) color terms containing an affix whose gloss is 'color, -colored, color of-', and so on, are more recent additions than those not containing such an affix;

    (v) color terms that are also the names (or contain the names) of objects characteristically having the color

in question are more recent additions than color
terms which are not (or do not contain) such a
name (see § 1.2).

If our evolutionary theory is correct, one would expect that
the terms acquired in Stage VII can be shown to be more recent than the Stage VI terms; that the term added at Stage VI
is more recent than those of Stage V, and so on. Terms at Stage
I should be the oldest in every language considered.

The evolutionary theory is generally corroborated when
principles of internal reconstruction are applied to our data.
In many of the Stage II systems reported, the term for RED
can be seen to be derived from the word for 'blood' [for example, Mid-Grand Valley Halyhalymo *mepmep* < *mep* 'blood'
(Bromley, 1967); Nasioi *esereŋ* 'red' < *ereŋ* 'blood' (Ogan, in
a personal communication); Queensland aborigines *ŏti* 'red' <
ŏti 'blood' (Rivers, 1901a)], while terms for BLACK and WHITE
lack known derivations.

The material presented by Rivers (1901a) for several of the
Torres Straits groups is interesting in this light. In the so-called
"Western Tribes" of this area, four of the six terms elicited as
being "names in general use" are formed by the use of a productive derivational suffix, *-dgamulnga* 'it looks like', plus the
name of some natural object. Thus we see *kulkadgamulnga* 'red
and purple' < *kulka* 'blood', *murdgamulnga* 'yellow and orange' < *mur* 'yellow ochre', *ildegamulnga* 'green and blue' <
il 'gall-bladder, bile', *maludgamulnga* 'blue and green' < *malu*
'sea'. The forms for 'black' and 'white' are less amenable to
analysis, Rivers being unsure of the derivation of 'white', that
is, *miakalunga* ~ *merkalunga* < *merkai?* 'spirit'. The term for
'black' *kubikubinga* is said to be derived from *kubi* 'charcoal,
night and darkness', but is formed by a distinctive derivational
principle, reduplication of the root plus *-nga*. It is likely that
the terms for 'black' and 'white' are older than the others, although we have no way of ordering the remaining terms. If we
accept Rivers' account that the latter are basic color terms, this
group must be classified as Stage IV or V. If, on the other hand,
they are descriptive phrases, as the internal evidence suggests,

then an assignment to Stage I is more appropriate. The latter interpretation is given some credence when Rivers states that "names for unfamiliar colours were apparently invented for the occasion by adding the usual suffix [that is, -dgamulnga] to the name of some natural object and once or twice a native omitted the termination and simply gave the name of the object" (1901a:59).

A comparable situation is seen in the language spoken on Murray Island, again drawing on Rivers' Torres Straits materials. Unlike the "Western Tribes" reported above, Murray Island color words are formed by "reduplication from the names of various natural objects" (1901a:56). Thus, we find *mammam* 'red' < *mam* 'blood', *bambam* 'orange, yellow' < *bam* 'turmeric', *siusiu* 'yellow' < *siu* 'yellow ochre', *sŏskĕpusŏskĕp* 'green' < *sŏskĕp* 'bile, gall-bladder', *bulubulu* 'blue' < English 'blue', *kakekakek* 'white' < ?, *golegole* 'black' < *gole* 'cuttlefish', *pipi* 'grey' < *pi* 'ashes'. The term for white was the only common expression for which Rivers found it impossible to obtain a derivation, and the derivation he offers for black is suspicious. By eliminating *bulubulu*, clearly an English loan, Murray Island might be interpreted, on internal evidence, as a Stage I system. That such an interpretation is plausible can be seen when Rivers notes, "It is interesting here that of the words in common use I only failed to obtain the derivations of the words for 'white' and of *sunursunur* and *akosakos*, meaning respectively 'bright' and 'dark or dull'. . . . All of the other names used for colours were found to be derived from natural objects which could be identified" (1901a:56).

One point should be made here concerning what might be considered incipient color categories and Rivers' contribution in this regard. While Rivers notes several times that "many of these . . . names were devised on the spur of the moment" (*ibid.*), he is nevertheless impressed by the high reliability of the more common descriptives. He suggests that this material may be taken as illustrative of vocabulary accretion in the domain of color, and that it should not be surprising when a new color category is linguistically recognized that it is labelled by the names of natural objects. Rivers concludes, "It is probable that when primitive man began to use names for colours, he used the names of natural objects either simply or modified in some way, and that definite generic terms have evolved out of these. The Mabuiag vocabulary [Western Torres Straits Tribe] is a good example of the coexistence of a large number of special names with a few which have become definitely abstract terms for colour [that is, black and white]" (1901a:63–64) . This fact is borne out in many languages where, for example, the word for red may be seen to have been derived from a form of the word for blood (Greenberg, 1963:154) .

The internal reconstruction for Swahili is interesting because it may be Stage II, having relatively old terms only for 'BLACK' *nyeusi*, 'WHITE' *nyeupe* and 'RED' *nyekundu*. The term for 'green' *kijani* may be new as it can be glossed 'leaf green'. The remaining terms are descriptives or loan words, that is, *kijivu* 'grey' < 'ashes', *chungwa* 'orange' < 'orange fruit', *khudhuru-ngi* 'brown' < Arabic 'brown', *kimanjano* 'yellow' < 'turmeric', *bulu* 'blue' < English 'blue', and *urujuani* 'purple' < Persian 'purple'.

Korean is an interesting example which illustrates the effect of foreign influence on the formulation of new color terminology. Korean has basic color terms (bound forms accompanied by a suffix meaning roughly 'color') for 'BLACK', 'WHITE', 'RED', 'GREEN', and 'YELLOW'. These expressions are clearly indigenous Korean forms. Terms for pink, orange, (chestnut) brown, brown, green, blue, purple, and grey, however, are of obvious Chinese derivation, as can be observed in the following forms. The Old Korean terms are: *kkamahta* 'BLACK', *hayahta* 'WHITE', *ppalkahta* 'RED', *nolahta* 'YELLOW', and *palahta* 'GREEN'. The Chinese loans are: *pwunhongsayk* 'pink', *tungsayk* 'orange', *kalsayk* 'brown', *pamsayk* '(chestnut) brown', *noksayk* 'green', *changsayk* 'blue', *casayk* 'purple', and *hoysayk* 'grey'.

Cantonese Chinese has also only recently reached Stage VII, judging by internal reconstruction of its color vocabulary. In dictionaries of one hundred years ago, the term for 'pink' *tsï* does not occur. The present meaning can be shown to be best translated as 'water colored'. The terms *luk* 'jade colored' and *l'ām* 'artifical blue' are also recent category labels which now segment GREEN. We may, therefore, reconstruct a Stage IV

Cantonese with the following terms: *pāk* 'WHITE', *hɒk* 'BLACK', *hung* 'RED', *ts'eng* 'GREEN', and *uong* 'YELLOW'.

That we find *fūi* 'grey' is somewhat anomalous. However, there is some evidence that it refers to 'ashes', and, if so, can be eliminated.

The appearance of new terms in some of the European languages is also indicative that, on internal evidence, these languages can be reconstructed to earlier stages. Bulgarian, for example, has borrowed terms *oranž* < French *orange, moravo* < (possible) Venetian *morado* 'purple'. Similarly, on internal evidence, the Hungarian terms *rózsaszín* 'pink', *barna* 'brown', *lila* 'purple' and *narancs* 'orange' appear to be late loans from Indo-European languages.

The term for blue, which appears at Stage V, is frequently a loan word. Rivers makes an interesting observation of this fact. He notes, "The English word [blue] has been borrowed by many African races, often taking the form of 'bru'. The Maoris use the English word changed into 'puru'. The Battas of Sumatra use the word 'balau' borrowed in a slightly modified form from the Dutch. They are also said to have borrowed the word 'biru' from the Malays, but this is probably a modification of the English word.[14] Some races in Borneo are said to use a word 'hidjan' borrowed from the Malay, and the Berbers are said to use a word 'samawi' (sky colour) borrowed from Arabic. The Hindustani word 'nil' is used for green and blue by several Asiatic peoples including the Tamils and Siamese.

"The Samoyeds sometimes use the Russian word 'sjinioi' for blue. In the Philippine Islands, the words used for green and blue by several tribes, such as the Ilocos, Tagals, and Bisayos, have been borrowed from the Spanish, and one of the Araucans of South America examined by Kirchhoff also called blue 'azul' " (1901a:67–68).

§ 2.5 *Problematical cases*

The vast majority of languages examined so far conform to our notions about the universality of color term foci as well as the evolutionary sequence of basic color terms. However, there are several problematical examples.

If we consider the questions raised by the sample of twenty languages for which we have experimental data, we note problems in the interpretation of Catalan, Cantonese, Mandarin, Japanese and Vietnamese. Catalan is clearly Stage VII but there appears to be some doubt, at least for the informant consulted, that the term for black is a basic, rather than secondary, color term. Corson (n.d.) reports that his Catalan informant realized that English 'black' was not a 'kind of grey' but consistently maintained that Catalan *negre* 'black' was a kind of *gris* 'grey'. This is the only example in our data where the status of black as a basic color term is questionable, and more data are clearly needed from additional Catalan speakers.

Our data from Cantonese and Mandarin Chinese present several problems in relation to the evolutionary hypothesis. We have treated Mandarin as an example of Stage V, with terms for black, white, RED, green, YELLOW and blue. There is also a term for grey which is the same as the word for 'ashes'. For one informant, who we later discovered is not a native speaker, (McClure, n.d.) this term is reported as basic; for several other informants (Madarasz, n.d.) grey is given as a tertiary form. Given these discrepancies, and the pattern pressure from the remaining data, we have treated Mandarin as Stage V and plan to obtain more data for this language in future research.

The problem with Cantonese is analogous. There exist terms for white, black, RED, green, YELLOW and blue (which would make it Stage V), but there are also terms for pink and grey. There is no term for brown, this category being included in yellow (Stross n.d.). There is reason to require more data for this language, however; several of the forms (pink, blue, grey) appear to be recent and their status as basic terms is as yet unclear.

Japanese also presents a problem in relation, not to its current state, but to its internal reconstruction. On the basis of internal evidence, the term for Japanese 'blue' *ao* is apparently of greater antiquity than 'green' *midori (iro)*. Moreover, there is some evidence that *ao* once was extended over greens and blues. If this is the case, we have a situation where the unitary term GREEN (at Stage IV) has its focal point in 'blue' and eventually reduces to blues exclusively with the later appearance of the term for green (at Stage V). If these conjectures are borne out by further work, we will have no alternative but to treat Japanese as a counterexample to the evolutionary sequence of the foci blue and green. However, alternative and equally plausible interpretations can be made which conform to the theory here presented. Final decision of the matter must await further research.

Vietnamese must be mentioned because it appears to lack a term for 'blue' but has basic terms for black, white, red, green, yellow, pink, purple, brown, and grey.

Turning to data derived from the literature and from personal communications, we note problems in the treatment of Western Apache, Hopi, Papago, all languages of the Southwestern United States; Samal, a Philippine language spoken off the Island of Mindanao; and Malay.

Materials from Western Apache (Keith Basso, in a personal communication) constitute an exception to the partial ordering of rule (1). A term for 'brown' ɬibaha appears contemporaneously with a unitary term for GREEN dukliž. In reference to the possible segmentation of dukliž 'GREEN', Basso notes "So far as I know this term, which covers a wide range of blues and greens, is not segmented linguistically at the basic color term level. Some referents include: the color of turquoise, which can range from light sky blue to rich 'Kelly' green; the color of all grasses . . . the color of all bush and tree leaves; the color of the eyes of an Appaloosa horse (perhaps the lightest blue there is) ; the color of an under-water algae . . . which is perhaps the darkest green." About the problem of whether the Western Apache term for brown ɬibaha is basic, Basso writes: "I believe that ɬibaha is unambiguously a basic color term, and best gloss I can come up with is 'brown'. Some referents: the color of sun-dried adobe bricks, actually a 'reddish brown' or 'rusty'; the color of the robes worn by early Lutheran missionaries (a 'most typical' brown form) ; the color of horses that you and I would refer to as 'bay'; the color of all leathers (treated or untreated) except for those dyed 'red', 'black' or one of the other basic colors that I described [above]" (ibid.).

Hopi (Voegelin and Voegelin, 1957) is analogous to Western Apache in that a sixth term is present while GREEN remains a unitary category including greens and blues. Unlike Apache's term for brown, Hopi includes a basic term for 'grey' *masí*. If grey proves to be a secondary form, Hopi will be a perfect Stage IV system.

Samal is problematical because Geoghegan, in a personal communication, reports *ʔabu* 'grey' as a basic color term, even though the expression is literally glossed 'ash'. If *ʔabu* eventually proves to be a descriptive, Samal will be classified as Stage V, with terms for black, white, red, green, yellow and blue.

Papago, as reported by K. Hale, in a personal communication, presents a similar problem. This language contains basic terms for white, black, red, yellow, green (including blue), and grey. If it were not for the presence of grey, Papago would be unequivocally Stage IV.

Malay and Bahasa Indonesia are Stage VII systems, lacking only a term for pink, and thus present no synchronic problem. However, the Stage VI and VII terms show a pattern of borrowing which does not fit the evolutionary sequence perfectly. 'Brown' is *tjokolat* (M) and *tjoklat* (I) < English or Dutch 'chocolate'. Similarly the forms *djinggo* (M) and *oranje* (I) 'orange' are obvious borrowings. Pink, as mentioned above, is absent. 'Grey' is *kelaboe* (M) and *kelabu* (I) < *abu* (M) 'ash'. However, we find for 'purple', *ongo* (M) and *ungu* (I) a simple root, attested also in Javanese (*wuŋu*), having apparently no meaning other than the abstract color term.

While internal reconstruction suggests that the purple term could be older than the brown term, such an interpretation is by no means necessary. The history of many language families, including Indo-European, shows that borrowing a foreign form for a basic color category may serve either to encode a previously uncoded perceptual category or to replace a native form. For example, the French form *bleu* was probably borrowed from Germanic for a previously uncoded category, while *blanc ~ blanche*, also of Germanic origin, almost certainly replaced a Romance form.[15]

In sum, of the ninety-eight languages considered, there is no counter-example to the finding of universality of the eleven color category foci, and there are just six serious candidates for counter-examples to the evolutionary ordering, which are: (a) the absence of brown in Cantonese; (b) the absence of blue in Vietnamese; (c) the presence of brown in Western Apache; and (d) the presence of grey in Hopi, Samal, and Papago (and possibly Mandarin).

The only systematic error, then, is the premature appearance of grey. If additional cases of this type are found the theory might have to be revised, perhaps by letting grey occur as a wild-card at various points in the evolutionary sequence, say at any point after Stage IV. Such a revision would have a certain plausibility as grey is exclusively a brightness term and thus might be partially immune to the constraints governing the progressive lexical partitioning of hue. However, we do not feel that three out of ninety-eight cases is a large enough number to justify a revision at this time.

§ 3 THE DATA

This section includes the data from the ninety-eight languages on which our analysis has been based. The materials presented here have been drawn from published sources and personal communications with linguists and ethnographers who have specialized knowledge of the languages in question. These data are summarized in Table III.

The order of presentation in this section is in terms of evolutionary stage, moving from Stage I sequentially through Stage VII. Ordering within stages is alphabetical by language name. (An alphabetical listing of all languages considered is found in Appendix III).

The following information is provided for each language considered:

Language name (as given in source) (Stage I, II, and so on)

Linguistic classification (Major family or stock and finer information where useful for purposes of identification)

Geographical area (continent and regional location)

Source (literature, personal communication, and so on)

Basic color terms (utilizing orthography and glosses of source)

Discussion (commentary, if any, on problems raised, general notes)

The first gloss given a form is the verbatim gloss of the source. Occasionally, we give a second gloss in square brackets [ ]; this is to be interpreted as suggested by § 2.2 and Note 12.

The linguistic classifications of these languages are taken from Voegelin and Voegelin (1957) unless otherwise indicated. They are intended solely as aids to identification of languages and not as contributions to historical linguistics.

§ *3.1 Languages exhibiting Stage I terminology*

We have data on nine languages with Stage I color terminology. In alphabetical order they are:

1. Dugum Dani (New Guinea)
2. Lower Valley Hitigima (New Guinea)
3. Jalé (New Guinea)
4. Murray Island (New Guinea)
5. Ngombe (Congo)
6. Paliyan (South India)
7. Pyramid-Wodo (New Guinea)
8. Upper Pyramid (New Guinea)
9. "Torres Straits Tribes" (New Guinea)

•

Language Dugum Dani (Stage I)
Linguistic class Central New Guinea, Ndani
Area New Guinea (West Highlands)
Source Heider (1965:170–171)
Basic color terms *modla* light, bright [WHITE]
mili dark, dull [BLACK]

Discussion "There are no other terms for color which are as non-object-specific as *modla* and *mili*. But there are a few rare terms which are used for more than one sort of object, and so might be considered true color terms. *Gut,* the name for the white heron, is also used to describe albinos. *Jagik,* the name for the cockatoo, is also used for a white clay. *Bima* (or sometimes *tet*) refers to the rusty color of some pigs, of the mountain dove, and to the ethnographer's beard. *Getega* refers to a bluish adze stone and to a greenish feather. *Hulu* may refer to bright red.

"These terms are sometimes used on the same level of contrast as *modla* and *mili*, but often, when pressed, informants would be uncertain. *Pima* (evidently a typographical error for *bima*) is most consistently used in direct contrast to *modla* and *mili* and comes the closest to being a color term in its own right" (Heider, 1965:170–171) .

●

Language	Lower Valley Hitigima (Stage I)
Linguistic class	Central New Guinea, Ndani
Area	New Guinea (Central Highlands)
Source	Bromley (1967:305–306)
Basic color terms	*mola* white, yellow, red [WHITE]
	muli black, green [BLACK]

Discussion For a discussion of two-term systems in this area, see § 2.3.1.

●

Language	Jalé (Stage I)
Linguistic class	Central New Guinea
Area	New Guinea (Central Highlands)
Source	Koch (personal communication)
Basic color terms	*hólo* light shades [WHITE]
	siŋ dark shades [BLACK]

Discussion Koch reports that other linguistic expressions denoting color are utilized by Jalé. However, these additional expressions invariably are also the names of specific natural objects or substances, for example, *mut* which may be used to refer to certain red-colored objects but whose basic reference is 'red soil'. The matter is discussed in greater detail in § 2.3.1.

●

Language	Murray Island (Stage I)
Linguistic class	non-Austronesian

Area New Guinea (Southeast coast)
Source Rivers (1901a:56)
Basic color terms *kakekakek* white [WHITE]
golegole black [BLACK]

Discussion In this group, color adjectives are formed primarily by "reduplication from the names of various natural objects" (Rivers, 1901a:56). Rivers is unable to determine the derivation of the term for 'white', and the derivation of *gole-gole* from *gole* 'cuttlefish' is suspicious. The remaining terms are descriptive, for example, *mammam* 'red' < *mam* 'blood'; *bambam* 'yellow, orange' < *bam* 'turmeric'; *siusiu* 'yellow' < *siu* 'yellow ochre'; *sŏskĕpusŏskĕp* 'green' < *sŏskĕp* 'bile, gall-bladder'; *bulubulu* 'blue' < English *blue;* and *pipi* 'grey' < *pi* 'ashes'.

●

Language Ngombe (Stage I)
Linguistic class Afro-asiatic, Chad group
Area Africa (Congo)
Source Stapleton (1903:225 ff.)
Basic color terms *bopu* white [WHITE]
bohindu black [BLACK]

Discussion In addition to the above terms, glossed simply as 'white' and 'black', Stapleton lists several additional expressions which appear to be descriptive. Each of these expressions is derived from the name of a natural object, to wit, "bokweto o ndondo *red, literally, the ripeness of red earth;* bopu o pembe, *a dull white, literally, the white of ivory;* bohindu okasa ngomu, *green,* literally *the blackness which seeks;* ngomu, *a fruit of the forest;* bohindu o malu, *dark blue, literally the blackness of charcoal;* light blue is reckoned green" (1903:255).

●

Language Paliyan (Stage I)
Linguistic class Dravidian, Tamil-Malayalam
Area South India
Source Gardner (1966a)

Basic color terms *velle* 'illuminated' (sometimes 'bright')
                    manja 'bright'
                    nīlam 'of medium brightness'
                    sihappu 'dark'
                    karuppu 'dark' or 'in shadow'

Discussion This interesting variant of Stage I is employed by a technologically marginal group in Southern India. Our data come from an unpublished manuscript by Peter M. Gardner (1966a), who recently returned from field work among these people. The Paliyans speak a dialect of Tamil, a major Dravidian language with about 30,000,000 speakers. An adjacent Tamil-speaking people, Plains Tamil, have a standard Stage V color terminology, given by Gardner as *vellai* 'white', *karuppu* 'black', *sivappu* 'red', *paccai* 'green', *manjal* 'yellow', and *nīlam* 'blue'.

In Paliyan Tamil, cognates of five of these six terms are retained, but with radically altered meanings. Discrimination is encoded exclusively in terms of brightness. Gardner's terminology is a bit unorthodox. He makes an analytical distinction between brightness due to intensity of light source (which he calls "illumination") and brightness due to properties of reflecting surface (which he calls "brightness"). He notes that the Paliyans classify these together on the dimension *niram,* 'brightness and illumination [sic]'. Paliyan color terms with their glosses and standard Plains Tamil sources are given below.

Paliyan		*Plains Tamil*
velle	'illuminated (sometimes 'bright')'	< *vellai* 'white'
manja	'bright'	< *manja* 'yellow'
nīlam	'of medium brightness'	< *nīlam* 'blue'
sihappu	'dark'	< *sivappu* 'red'
karuppu	'dark' or 'in shadow'	< *karuppu* 'black'

Gardner indicates that there is considerable overlap in usage between each term in the Paliyan series and its neighbors. The effect on the usage of the terms of the extent to which brightness comes from light source as opposed to surface properties is not entirely clear from Gardner's preliminary manuscript.

The most extreme terms, *veḷḷe* and *karuppu,* are not reserved exclusively for the extremes of brightness. Gardner says "The usual leaf on a tree is *veḷḷe* on its upper surface and *karuppu* on its lower surface" (1966a). He also notes, however, that the same leaf may well be *nīlam* or *sihappu* (presumably on both sides) if seen in different light.

In any case, whether or not Paliyan can be construed as a perfect example of a Stage I color lexicon, it is certainly a variant of this basic type. Gardner's statements support this view. For example, "*sihappu* was elicited for dark shades of red, yellow, green, purple and black" (1966a).

Of particular interest for the evolutionary hypothesis is Gardner's conviction that these people have a minimum of shared culture. He speaks of "imprecision and lack of elaboration in the most basic aspects of Paliyan subsistence related classifications . . . highly idiosyncratic taxonomy . . . de-emphasis on both verbal communication and formality of expression [sic]" (1966a; see also Gardner 1966b:397–399).

The Paliyan data invite another speculation, plausible but lacking in direct support. Several lines of evidence, including distinct physical differences between Paliyans and Plains Tamil speakers, indicate that the Paliyans may at one time have spoken a language unrelated to Tamil (and perhaps to any other extant language). Parallels can be seen in the loss of their native language of various Pigmoid groups, for example, the acceptance of Bantu by the Pigmies of the Central Congo. We may speculate that the original language of the Paliyans contained terms for BLACK and WHITE, that is, for two degrees of brightness *(niram)*. In learning Tamil, the Paliyans encountered additional terms for the quality of reflected light and simply accepted the Plains Tamil meanings as far as the dimension of brightness was concerned. Note that the Paliyan terms for the extremes of brightness are cognate with the Plains Tamil terms for white and black; that the Paliyan terms for secondary degrees of brightness and darkness are respectively the Plains Tamil terms for yellow and red (note in Figures 1 and 3 that yellow and red are the brightest and darkest of the basic categories other than white and black) ; and that whereas Plains Tamil lacks a term for grey, blue is taken in Paliyan as the middle-brightness category. (Note in Figure 3 that blue is *par excellence* the middle-brightness category other than grey.)

●

    Language Pyramid-Wodo (Stage I)
Linguistic class Central New Guinea, Ndani
    Area New Guinea (Central Highlands)
    Source Bromley (1967:305–306)
Basic color terms moδa white, red, yellow [WHITE]
    muδi black [BLACK]

Discussion Bromley indicates a third term, *getega*, for 'green'. However, the term is analyzable into *get* 'fresh' and *ega* 'leaf'. Elsewhere, Bromley (1967:288) indicates that the expression is best treated as a descriptive phrase and not as a basic color term. (See also the discussion in § 2.3.1.)

●

    Language Upper Pyramid (Stage I)
Linguistic class Central New Guinea, Ndani
    Area New Guinea (Central Highlands)
    Source Bromley (1967:305, 306)
Basic color terms mola white, red, yellow [WHITE]
    muli black, dark green [BLACK]

Discussion See again the discussion of Dani systems in § 2.3.1.

●

    Language "Torres Straits Tribes", on the islands of Mabuig, Muralag, Badu, Moa and Saibai (Stage I)
Linguistic class Australian, Poma-Nyungan, Mabuiagic
    Area New Guinea (Southeast coast)
    Source Rivers (1901a:59)
Basic color terms miakalunga ~ merkalunga white [WHITE]
    kubikubinga black [BLACK]

Discussion There appear to be six terms in this area which refer to color and which Rivers claims to be "names in general use." Four of these expressions are derived from the name of some natural object plus a productive suffix, *-dga-*

mulnga, most appropriately glossed as 'it looks like'. Thus, we see *kulkadgamulnga* 'red and purple' < *kulka* 'blood'; *murdgamulnga* 'yellow and orange' < *mur* 'yellow ochre'; *ildegamulnga* 'green and blue' < *il* 'gall-bladder, bile'; *maludgamulnga* 'blue and green' < *malu* 'sea'. As we have indicated in § 2.3.1, we interpret only the terms for 'black' and 'white' as basic and treat the remainder as descriptive expressions. This interpretation is in agreement with Rivers, who notes that "names for unfamiliar colours were apparently invented for the occasion by adding the usual suffix to the name of some natural object and once or twice a native omitted the termination and simply gave the name of the object" (1901a:59). See also § 2.4.

§ 3.2 Languages exhibiting Stage II terminology

We have data on twenty-one languages with Stage II color systems. They are:

1. Arawak (Surinam)
2. Baganda (Uganda)
3. Bambara (French Sudan)
4. Bantu (Congo)
5. Bullom (Sierra Leone)
6. Bulu (Africa)
7. Jekri (Nigeria)
8. Kongo [sic] (Congo)
9. Lingala (Africa)
10. Nasioi (Bougainville)
11. Ndembu (Congo)
12. Pomo (United States)
13. Poto (Congo)
14. "Queensland" (Queensland, Australia)
15. Shona (Rhodesia)
16. Swahili (Tanzania)
17. Tiv (Nigeria)
18. Toda (South India)
19. Tonga (Mozambique)
20. Tshi (West Africa)
21. Yibir (Chad)

Language dialect of Arawak (=Lokono?) (Stage II)
Linguistic class Andean-Equatorial, Equatorial, Arawakan
Area South America (Surinam)
Source van Wijk (1959:128, 130)
Basic color terms *a-li* white, light shades [WHITE]
           o-ri dark shades, bluish and brownish black
           [BLACK]
           kore reddish and gold-like shades, maize color
           [RED]

Discussion Van Wijk's glosses of the Arawak terms are
drawn from the work of de Goeje (1928). These data are
somewhat questionable, but van Wijk appears confident that
the Arawak system is one based on simple brightness distinctions.

●

Language Baganda (Stage II)
Linguistic class Congo-Kordofanian, Niger-Congo, Benue-
           Congo branch
Area Africa (Uganda, N.W. Lake Victoria)
Source van Wijk (1959:128, 130)
Basic color terms *eru* light shades, yellow, beige, light blue
           [WHITE]
           dagaru dark shades, dark blue, black [BLACK]
           mynfu reddish shades, pink, orange, brown,
           purple [RED]

Discussion Van Wijk's original source for Baganda is
Simon (1951) who studied this group for color blindness.

●

Language Bambara (Stage II)
Linguistic class Congo-Kordofanian, Niger-Congo, Mende,
           Western
Area Africa (SW French Sudan [sic])
Source van Wijk (1959:128, 130)
Basic color terms *dyéma* white, beige, naturel [sic] [WHITE]
           fima dark-green, indigo, black [BLACK]
           bléma reddish and brownish shades [RED]

Discussion Van Wijk draws his Bambara materials from Zahan (1951). He notes that Zahan "gives only three 'color' terms, but states that each is also applied to a number of other colours, which to us would not seem very much alike; for instance, there is one term [*fima*] for dark green, indigo and black" (1959:130).

☺

Language Bantu (Stage II)
Linguistic class Congo-Kordofanian,   Niger-Congo,   Benue-Congo, Bantoid
Area Africa (Congo)
Source Rivers (1901a:90)
Basic color terms ____ white [WHITE]
    ____ black [BLACK]
    ____ red [RED]

Discussion Rivers, in his discussion of Buchner's work published in 1883, notes that the Bantu described "have only three words for colours, one for black, which means also blue, one for white, which also means yellow and light, and one for red" (1901a:90). The native forms are not cited by Rivers. We have not been able to obtain Buchner's work.

●

Language Bullom (Stage II)
Linguistic class Congo-Kordofanian, Niger-Congo, West Atlantic
Area Africa (Sierra Leone)
Source Nylander (1814:123, 134, 147, 158, 159)
Basic color terms *linteh ~ dinteh* white [WHITE]
    të black [BLACK]
    shah red [RED]

Discussion Nylander lists the term *shaw* for 'yellow'. It seems clear on phonetic grounds that this is the same term as *shah* 'red'. An expression for 'green, unripe' *buttul* occurs but does not refer to the color. Finally, a term for 'blue', *te* is listed (also alternative *rokeh*) which is probably the same term as *të* cited for 'black'.

•

Language	Bulu (Stage II)
Linguistic class	Congo-Kordofanian, Niger-Congo, Benue-Congo, Bantoid
Area	Africa
Source	von Hagen (1914)
Basic color terms	*fum* white [WHITE]
	vin black [BLACK]
	re red [RED]

•

Language	Jekri (Stage II)
Linguistic class	Congo-Kordofanian, Niger-Congo, Kwa Branch
Area	Africa (Nigeria, Delta region)
Source	Granville and Granville (1898:104–126)
Basic color terms	*fufé* white [WHITE]
	dudu black [BLACK]
	dĭdé red [RED]

Discussion The authors note: "The word *égo* [green] is not used by itself, thus to say *egĭ* (tree), *égo* (green), a green tree would not be understood; one must say *egi to mu égo* literally 'tree which catch green'. Paint is known by the name applied to tar *ŏda*. To say 'green paint', they say *ŏda to mu égo* 'tar which catch green', but for red paint they say *ŏda dĭdé* tar red" (1898:123–124).

•

Language	Kongo [sic] (Stage II)
Linguistic class	Congo-Kordofanian, Niger-Congo, Benue-Congo
Area	Africa (Congo)
Source	Stapleton (1903:255)

Basic color terms mpɛ́mbɛ́ white [WHITE]
ndombe black [BLACK]
mbwaki red [RED]

Discussion These are the only three color expressions
that Stapleton reports as basic color terms. The other terms
"are described by reference to some well known object, thus,
—elundu, *a very light brown,* lit. *an anthill;* knogo, *a darker
brown,* lit. *a wood ground to make a cosmetic;* ti kiangiu,
green, lit. *green grass;* ndua, *purple, the colour of the breast
of bird* ndua; ntoto a egenda, *yellow,* lit. *the soil in a chasm.*
Dark blue is called black; and light blue, green; orange is red;
and violet black" (1903:255).

•

Language Lingala (Stage II)
Linguistic class Congo-Kordofanian,   Niger-Congo,   Benue-
Congo, Bantoid
Area Africa
Source Anderson (n.d.)
Basic color terms mpɛ́mbɛ́ white [WHITE]
mwindo black [BLACK]
motáné red [RED]

Discussion Anderson's knowledge derives from his father
who has done mission work among the Lingala.

•

Language Nasioi (Stage II)
Linguistic class Southern Bougainville
Area South Pacific (Bougainville)
Source Ogan (personal communication)
Basic color terms kakara white [WHITE]
mutaŋa black, dark [BLACK]
erereŋ red [RED]

Discussion Ogan notes that *erereŋ* is clearly derived from
ereŋ 'blood', but finds no etymologies for the terms for BLACK
and WHITE. Commenting on additional terms found in Rausch
(1912), Ogan notes the following:

"*tikatikaŋ* 'schwarz'—I never heard this word used by the Nasioi. When I read the word aloud and asked them about it, they would laugh and reply *nii,* 'us', i.e., black people. (They also refer to themselves as *mutaŋa.*)

"*itaku,* 'dunkel wie ein Wald' (dark like a forest) in contrast to *mutaŋa* 'das Dunkel der Nacht' (the darkness of night). I cannot now check this out, but I feel that I never heard *itaku* used and, if I asked about it, got a reply referring to *pora,* 'the bush, jungle'.

"*kapika,* 'grün'—This word means 'green' only in the sense of 'unripe'; also, 'raw, uncooked'.

"On the few occasions I asked about color words, pointing to the specific objects I perceived as blue or green, informants replied *paniŋ pina oro,* 'looks like the sky', or *ba pino oro* 'looks like a leaf'. Younger people would also respond with English or pidgin, 'blue or blupela' " (personal communication). (See also the discussion of Nasioi in § 2.3.2.)

•

Language Ndembu (Stage II)
Linguistic class Congo-Kordofanian, Niger-Congo, Benue-
          Congo
Area Africa (Congo)
Source Turner (1966:48, 58, 60)
Basic color terms *tooka* white [WHITE]
          wuyila blackness [BLACK]
          ku-chinana to be red (or yellow) [RED]

Discussion Turner presents one of the most extended discussions of the ritual significance of color in the recent literature. His discussion of the Ndembu color vocabulary is cited in § 2.3.2.

•

Language Pomo (Stage II)
Linguistic class Hokan
Area United States (California)
Source Corson (n.d.)
Basic color terms *tótokin* white [WHITE]
          likolkokin black [BLACK]
          tantankin red [RED]

Discussion This is one of the twenty languages for which we have experimental data. See Appendix I for a full treatment.

•

Language	Poto (Stage II)
Linguistic class	Congo-Kordofanian, Niger-Congo, Benue-Congo
Area	Africa (Congo)
Source	Stapleton (1903:255)
Basic color terms	*botani* white [WHITE]
	boindu black [BLACK]
	eyeyengo yellow [sic] [RED]

Discussion In his discussion of the remaining color expressions in Poto, nowhere does Stapleton give a simple term for red. The structual characteristics of the several other languages that he describes (Kongo, Bangi, Ngombe, Swahili) indicate strongly that a color term for red is present. We surmise that *eyeyengo* is most likely the Poto term for 'RED' encompassing, as Stapleton notes in his gloss, 'yellow'. The following additional expressions are noted: "Boindu wa lombi-lombi, *a bright blue*, lit. *the black of a stick which has a bright surface;* botani wa ngola, *red*, lit. *the white of camwood;* botani wa fe, a dull blue. Fe is a root signifying *sickly, thin, poverty-stricken;* a dull blue is a sickly black, or, as my informant says, a black which has failed to be black" (1903:255).

•

Language	Queensland (Stage II)
Linguistic class	non-Austronesian
Area	Australia (Queensland, Gulf of Carpentaria)
Source	Rivers (1901a:87–88)
Basic color terms	*yŏpa, wăpŏk* white, yellow, green [WHITE]
	unma, manara black, blue, indigo, violet [BLACK]
	ŏti, owang red, purple, orange [RED]

Discussion As mentioned in § 2.3.2, *ŏti* is also "said to be the word for blood . . ." (1901a:88) and, as such, may not be a basic color term. If this is so, then the Queensland group might best be treated as Stage I.

•

Language Shona (Dialect A) (Stage II)
Linguistic class Congo-Kordofanian, Niger-Congo, Benue-Congo
Area Africa (Rhodesia)
Source Gleason (1961:45)
Basic color terms   *cicena* white, green, yellow [WHITE]
                      citema black, blue [BLACK]
                      *cips*ᵘuka* red, purple, orange [RED]

Discussion According to Gleason (1961:429), "The Shona group of dialects occupies a large part of Rhodesia and adjacent Portuguese East Africa. There are six reasonably clearly marked groups of dialects, each showing appreciable local variation." Gleason does not specify which Shona dialect is represented by these color terms. It is clearly distinct from the dialect of Shona studied by Goldberg (n.d.), who also, unfortunately, fails to identify her dialect (a Stage IV language). The Shona dialect studied by Goldberg is discussed in § 3.4, where it is designated 'Shona (Dialect B)'.

•

Language Swahili (Stage II)
Linguistic class Congo-Kordofanian, Niger-Congo, Benue-Congo
Area Africa (upcountry Swahili, Tanzania)
Source Stapleton (1903:255), van Wijk (1959:128, 130)
          Madarasz (n.d.)
Basic color terms -*eupe* white (Stapleton) ⎤
                meupe white and light shades ⎟
                    (van Wijk) ⎬ [WHITE]
                nyeupe white (Madarasz) ⎦

-*eusi* black (Stapleton)
neusi black, dark shades (van Wijk) } [BLACK]
nyeusi black (Madarasz)

ekundu red (Stapleton)
nyekundu reddish shades, orange, rose, brown (van Wijk) } [RED]
nyekundu red (Madarasz)

Discussion Swahili is one of the twenty languages for which we have systematically collected data (Madarasz n.d.). In this research, Swahili appears to exhibit color terminology which would indicate a Stage VII classification. Many of the linguistic expressions, however, appear to be foreign loan words or are descriptive in nature. The almost identical terms and glosses given by Stapleton (1903:255) and van Wijk (1959:128, drawing upon the work of Simon [1951]) would suggest that Swahili is actually a simpler system exhibiting only three basic color terms. We have, accordingly, placed Swahili at Stage II. See § 2.4 for further discussion. Swahili is mapped in Appendix I, page 128.

●

Language Tiv (Stage II)
Linguistic class Congo-Kordofanian, Niger-Congo, Benue-Congo, Bantoid
Area Africa (Nigeria)
Source Bohannan (1963:35–36)
Basic color terms *pupu* very light blues, light greys, white [WHITE]
ii green, some blues, some greys, dark colors black [BLACK]
nyian all warm colors through red to yellow, brown [RED]

Discussion Tiv has been discussed and diagrammed in the text (see § 2.3.2, also Note 1). It is worthwhile to reiterate here that "The distinction between *ii* [BLACK] and *pupu* [WHITE] is not in terms of color, but in terms of what we would call shade—darkness and lightness" (1963:35).

●

Language Toda (Stage II)
Linguistic class Dravidian, Tamil-Malayalam
Area South India
Source Rivers (1905:327)
Basic color terms *pelthiti* it is white [WHITE]
kârthiti it is black [BLACK]
pògh red, blood, orange [RED]

Discussion Rivers notes that yellow is labelled by the Canarese loan *ârsena*. "Thus [*ârsena*] is probably not a true Toda word but borrowed from Canarese through intercourse with the Badagas. Green received many names, including *ers,* leaf; *òmadi,* moss; *pachai,* the Tamil word for green; *nîl,* blue and *kâg,* dark or black. Blue and indigo were called *nîl* most frequently but also *kâg* or *kârthiti,* black. The nomenclature for violet was very indefinite; some could not give it a name; others compared it to some natural object, and others called it *nîl* or *kâri,* charcoal. The nomenclature for brown was equally indefinite. Papers of different shades of brown were named by the majority after some variety of earth or were compared to sticks, leaves, skin, soot, beeswax, etc., and were occasionally called black, white, or yellow. It was quite clear that there was no generic word for brown. White was unanimously called *pelthiti* ('it is white') and black was called *kârthiti* ('it is black') or *kâg* or *kâri.* Different greys were usually called *pelthiti* if light or *kârthiti* if dark; a few people called light grey *pûthi,* ashes, a form of the common South Indian word for this colour.

"In 1880, Magnus on the authority of a missionary, described the Todas and other Nilgiri tribes as having a definite colour word only for red. [Magnus was not considering the terms for 'black' and 'white' as "color" words]. If the borrowed words, *ârsena* and *nîl,* be excluded, it is still correct to say that red is the only colour for which the Todas have one term used with any degree of unanimity, but they are nevertheless able to name other colours by means of words of which the derivation shows that they are used suitably and that the colour has been discriminated" (1905:327).

●

Language Tonga (Stage II)
Linguistic class Congo-Kordofanian, Niger-Congo, Benue-Congo
Area Africa (Southern Mozambique)
Source Colson (personal communication)
Basic color terms *čituba* white and all light colors [WHITE]
čisia black and all dark colors [BLACK]
čisubila red, including oranges and dark yellows [RED]

Discussion The dialect of Shona described earlier by Gleason (1961:4) appears to be closely related to that of Colson's Tonga people. Note that the apparent cognate pairs *citema/čituba* and *cicena/čisia* suggest that the glosses for the forms may have been interchanged in Gleason's account.

●

Language Tshi (Stage II)
Linguistic class unclassified
Area Africa (West Africa)
Source Rivers (1901a:90)
Basic color terms *fufu* white [WHITE]
tuntum black [BLACK]
koko red [RED]

Discussion Rivers draws his data on Tshi from Riis's work published in 1853. We have not located the original source.

●

Language Yibir (Stage II)
Linguistic class Afro-Asiatic, Cushitic, Eastern
Area Africa (Southeastern Chad)
Source Kirk (1905:207, 211, 213)
Basic color terms *iftin* white [WHITE]
humǎksan black [BLACK]
ásèrah red [RED]

Discussion According to Kirk, Yibir is a secret language spoken by one of the two outcast tribes living among the Somalis and known to them as *Sab* 'outcast'. In his comparative vocabulary of Yibir and Somali, these terms appear as the only color terms for Yibir.

§ 3.3 *Languages exhibiting Stage III terminology*

Our materials to date show eight languages with Stage IIIa terms and nine with Stage IIIb terms, a total of seventeen. They are, by substage, as follows:

IIIa systems
  1. Bagirmi   (Chad)
  2. Hanunóo   (Philippines)
  3. Ibibio   (Nigeria)
  4. Ila   (Africa)
  5. Mende   (Sierra Leone)
  6. Poul   (Africa)
  7. Somali   (Chad)
  8. Tanna Island   (Torres Straits)

IIIb systems
  1. Arunta   (Australia)
  2. Bisayan   (Philippines)
  3. Ellice Island   (Polynesia)
  4. "Fitzroy River"   (Australia)
  5. Greek (Homeric)   (Mediterranean)
  6. Ibo   (Nigeria)
  7. Pukapuka   (Polynesia)
  8. Tongan   (Polynesia)
  9. Urhobo   (Nigeria)

●

Language Bagirmi (Stage IIIa)
Linguistic class Nilo-Saharan, Chari-Nile, Central Sudanic
Area Africa (Chad)
Source Gaden (1909:113, 134, 141, 146)
Basic color terms *dap/e* blanc [WHITE]
                 il/i noir [BLACK]
                 'at'e rouge [RED]
                 katarpo bleu, vert [GREEN]

Discussion Gaden gives no indication of the maximal extensions of these expressions.

•

Language	Hanunóo (Stage IIIa)
Linguistic class	Austronesian, Hanunoic
Area	Philippines (Mindoro)
Source	Conklin (1955), van Wijk (1959:128–130)
Basic color terms	(*ma*) *lagti?* white, light tints of other colors [WHITE]
	(*ma*) *biru* black, violet, indigo, blue, dark green, dark grey and deep shades of other colors [BLACK]
	(*ma*) *rara?* maroon, red, orange, yellow [RED]
	(*ma*) *latuy* green, mixtures of green, yellow and light brown [GREEN]

Discussion Conklin's classic work on the ethnographic description of color is best known for demonstrating the importance of non-colorimetric components (in this case succulence and desiccation) as relevant semantic features of color words. Hanunóo may nonetheless be characterized as a Stage IIIa system. (See also Note 2.)

•

Language	Ibibio (Stage IIIa)
Linguistic class	Congo-Kordofanian, Niger-Congo, Benue-Congo branch, Cross River
Area	Africa (South Nigeria)
Source	E. Kaufman (n.d.)
Basic color terms	àfíá [WHITE]
	èɓuɓit [BLACK]
	ǹdàídàt [RED]
	àwàwà [GREEN]

Discussion Ibibio is included as one of our original twenty languages. It is diagrammed in Figure 13A; the original mapping is shown in Appendix I.

•

Language Ila (Stage IIIa)
Linguistic class Congo-Kordofanian, Niger-Congo, Benue-Congo
Area Africa
Source Smith (1907:269, 273, 301, 331, 353)
Basic color terms *ku tuba* to be white [WHITE]
ku shia to be black [BLACK]
ku subila to be red [RED]
itubuzhu green [GREEN]

Discussion We have conservatively classified Ila as Stage IIIa but it is very likely a Stage II system on simple inspection of the basic color terms. Terms are also cited for two shades of brown which appear to be derived forms; that is, *ifumbalushi* 'light brown' perhaps < *ifūmbo* 'fruit of the *munto koshia* tree'; *ishīshī* 'dark brown' perhaps < *ishi* 'quantity of smoke'. We are not treating these expressions for brown as basic color terms.

•

Language Mende (Stage IIIa)
Linguistic class Congo-Kordofanian, Niger-Congo, Mende branch, Western
Area Africa (Sierra Leone)
Source Migeod (1908:128)
Basic color terms *kole* white [WHITE]
teli black [BLACK]
kpou red, brown [RED]
pune green [GREEN]

Discussion Migeod, in his discussion of Mende color adjectives, also includes *bulw* 'blue', which appears clearly to be derived from English blue. There is also a term *ngañpu* which refers to any object of variegated color.

•

Language Poul (=Poular?) (Stage IIIa)
Linguistic class Congo-Kordofanian, Niger-Congo, West Atlantic, Fulani

Area Africa (West Africa)
Source Faidherbe (1882:129, 149, 156, 161)
Basic color terms *danédjo, ranébé* blanc [WHITE]
balédjio, balébé noir [BLACK]
goddioudo, hoddioubé rouge [RED]
gobou, goboudji vert, bleu [GREEN]

Discussion Faidherbe provides no discussion of the extension of these terms.

●

Language Somali (Stage IIIa)
Linguistic class Afro-Asiatic (Eastern Cushitic)
Area Africa (Southeastern Chad)
Source Kirk (1905), de Larajasse (1897)
Basic color terms *'ad* white [WHITE] (Kirk)
mado black [BLACK] (Kirk)
madow black [BLACK] (de Larajasse)
'as red [RED] (Kirk)
owlaled green [GREEN] (de Larajasse)

Discussion The data on Somali are ambiguous in several respects and our interpretation of this group as Stage IIIa should therefore be considered tentative. Kirk (1905) and de Larajasse (1897) are in total agreement as to the presence of terms for 'white' *'ad,* 'black' *mado* or *madow* and 'red' *'as* in Somali. Only de Larajasse reports an adjectival term for 'green' *owlaled* (1897:115). The adjective glossed as 'yellow' in Kirk (1905:38) is *'aul.* In de Larajasse this term (*'aul*) is glossed "m[asculine] and f[eminine] n[oun], gazelle (Gasella Soemmeringi) " (1897:12). De Larajasse does list a term for 'yellow color', *wob,* but it is classified as a masculine noun and not as an adjective. The term for 'blue' in de Larajasse is *madow 'adan* literally 'black whiteness'. Finally, de Larajasse includes two entries for 'brown'. One is *marrin,* classified as a masculine noun. The second form, *owlan* is classified as an adjective meaning 'brown, reddish' and is a derivative of the form for 'green' *owlaled.*

The following interpretation of these data allows us to treat

Somali as Stage IIIa: (1) de Larajasse includes a term for 'green' which is a legitimate adjectival form; (2) the term for 'yellow' is rejected because (a) the two sources disagree as to the glossing of *'aul,* and (b) the term *wob* is a noun and *not* an adjective as are terms for white, black, red, and green; (3) terms for blue and brown are rejected as either (a) nouns or (b) descriptive or derived expressions.

•

Language	Tanna Island (Stage IIIa)
Linguistic class	non-Austronesian
Area	Coastal New Guinea-Australia (Torres Straits)
Source	Rivers (1901a:85)
Basic color terms	*ratuan* white [WHITE]
	rapen black [BLACK]
	laulau red [RED]
	ramimera green [GREEN]

Discussion Several terms which appear to be simple modifications of the above basic forms are discussed in § 2.3.3.

•

Language	Arunta (Stage IIIb)
Linguistic class	Australian
Area	Australia
Source	Spencer and Gillen (1927:552–553)
Basic color terms	*churunkura* white [WHITE]
	urapulla black [BLACK]
	tutuka red [RED]
	tierga (turga) yellow, green, blue [YELLOW]

Discussion "The Arunta native has distinctive names for only four colours: red is *tutuka,* white is *churunkura,* black is *urapulla,* yellow is *tierga* (or *turga*), the same word [that is, *tierga*] being also used for green and blue. . . . He calls red ochre *ulpa* or *perta tutuka;* yellow ochre *upla* or *perta tierga;* white pipeclay *perta churunkura;* or a red leaf *ilpilla tutuka;* a green or yellow leaf *ilpilla tierga;* lime, or limestone, *erulla* (earth) *willia* (soft) *churunkura* (white) ; charcoal *purka;* blue sky *alkira tierga tierga.* An Arunta is now called *mberga urapulla;* a white man *mberga churunkura.*

"His appreciation of colours has, of necessity, been limited to those four pigments available to him. Just as amongst flowers, blue is the highest and latest to be developed, so, amongst human beings, blue seems to have been the latest pigment discovered and appreciated, and it was never used by any Australian savage. There is no natural blue pigment available to him amongst the materials forming part of his environment. The nearest approach to it is wad, a manganese ore only rarely met with, which, when powdered, has a bluish-grey tint, for which he uses the same name as for black. It is not simply a case of his having one word to describe two or three colours which, in reality, he regards as different from one another. He does not, apparently, distinguish the one from the other. It is somewhat difficult to express this matter accurately. If, for example, an Arunta native is shown black, brown, and grey objects, such as skeins of wool or coloured cardboard, he will apply the same colour term to each of them. On the other hand, if shown an object of a particular shade of colour, such as that of his own skin, and asked to match this with one of three or four shades of chocolate brown, he will, after consideration, usually decide upon the correct one. Black and all varieties of brown and grey are, apparently, only what we call "shades" or the same colour, indistinguishable to him from one another, unless placed side by side" (Spencer and Gillen, 1927:552–553) . We would not now consider the latter conclusion justified by the evidence cited.

•

Language Bisayan (Stage IIIb)
Linguistic class Austronesian, Tagalic, Bisayan
Area Philippines (Leyte Island)
Source Kepner (1905:680–683)
Basic color terms *mabosag* white [WHITE]
maitum black [BLACK]
mapula red [RED]
madarag yellow [YELLOW]

Discussion In a discussion of Bisayan color perception, Kepner presents sufficient data to establish this system as Stage IIIb before the arrival of the Spanish. From the Spanish, the Bisayans had borrowed the word for blue, *azul*, utilizing it for both 'blue' and 'green'. For example, when a girl was asked the color of a handkerchief that she wore around her neck, Kepner reports: "She answered correctly that it was blue. But to the next question she replied that the grass was the same color." In addition, "Another girl . . . pronounced a rather dark green leaf *maitum*—black . . . dark blue was also called 'black'. A class of thirteen girls in the same school . . . named properly and without any difficulty the colors of pencils painted red and yellow. But the green and blue pencils they could not at all name" (1905:682).

The use of the Spanish *azul* to describe both blue and green would suggest that the Bisayans were moving out of Stage IIIb when they first came into contact with Spanish speakers. The area of blues and greens was an incipient color category for which a name had not yet been encoded. Compare, now, the discussion of Tzeltal *yaš*, § 2.3.4.

•

Language Ellice Island (Vaitupu) (Stage IIIb)
Linguistic class Austronesian, West Polynesian, Ellicean
Area Polynesia
Source Kennedy (1931)
Basic color terms *kena* white, light-coloured [WHITE]
     uli black, dark-coloured [BLACK]
     kula flame-coloured, any shade of red or brown [RED]
     senga colour of a dead leaf; light brown, yellowish [YELLOW]

Discussion Kennedy's remarks echo those of Magnus and Rivers, cited elsewhere, in showing that systems of Stages II and III tend to retain Stage I usage in many contexts. Kennedy opens his section entitled Colour-Sense and Colour Names as follows: "It would seem that the only true colour distinctions are between white or light-coloured and black or dark-coloured. A dark shade of almost any colour would be called

uli [BLACK] (e.g., *Tefea te lupe? Tela e uli mai i ti lakau*—
'where is the pigeon?' 'There in the tree, it appears dark'. Lit.
'it blacks toward us')" (1931:102).

●

Language	"Fitzroy River" group (Stage IIIb)
Linguistic class	Australian
Area	Australia (Queensland coast)
Source	Rivers (1901a:89)
Basic color terms	*bura* white [WHITE]
	guru black, blue, indigo [BLACK]
	kiran red, purple [RED]
	kalmur yellow, green, orange, blue-green [GREEN]
Discussion	See § 2.3.3.

●

Language	Greek (Homeric) (Stage IIIb)
Linguistic class	Indo-European, Greek
Area	Europe
Source	Capell (1966:40)
Basic color terms	*lɛukɔ́s* snow, water, sun, metallic surface, bright, shining, brilliant, clear [WHITE]
	glaukɔ́s eye-color, willow, olive, sedge [BLACK]
	ɛrythrɔ́s rtd, blood-color, copper color, wine or nectar [RED]
	khlɔ:rɔ́s green, yellow tints, young leaves, honey sand [YELLOW]

Discussion As indicated in Note 6, Gladstone (1858) and
Geiger (1880) were both convinced that many of the classical
languages, especially Homeric Greek, lacked color terms in the
modern sense. See also Appendix III. Capell (1966), in commenting on discrepancy of color nomenclature in the languages of the world, also notes the paucity of color words in
Ancient Greek. Thus, "the colour system of Ancient Greek is
not strictly commensurable with that of modern English and
modern European in general. Some examples may be given:

(1) In Homer, Hera is described as 'grey eyed' in some standard translations, and the word glaukɔ́s is normally applied to eye-color, but it also describes the willow, the olive and the sedge, none of which has anything in common with eyes in color. The word originally had no reference to color but meant 'bleaming, glancing', and then 'silvery'. (2) ɛrythrɔ́s, used for 'red', 'blood color', 'copper color' is really 'like wine or nectar'. (3) lɛukɔ́s is applied to snow, water, sun or metallic surface or fair skin; its significance was really 'bright', 'shining', 'brilliant' or 'clear'. (4) khlɔːrɔ́s was applied to green and yellow tints, such as young leaves, honey and sand: it is radically 'pale'. Whenever a color is definitely specified, as in kýanɔs 'dark blue', it is usually a metaphorical transfer: kýanɔs is the lapis lazuli first of all. In other words, Greek color terminology was concerned with shades, not with color in the modern artistic sense" (1966:40).

We are inclined to treat this lexicon as Stage IIIb in terms of the glosses provided by Capell. Further work remains to be done in order to determine the essential correctness of Gladstone's belief that the Greek of Homeric times actually had terms only for "dark" and "light" shades.

Note: The orthography employed here for Homeric Greek is Capell's.

•

           Language Ibo (Stage IIIb)
    Linguistic class Congo-Kordofanian, Niger-Congo, Kwa
              Area Africa (Nigeria)
         Source Goldberg (n.d.)
Basic color terms *nzu* white, grey [WHITE]
                 oji black [BLACK]
                 uhie red, dull red [RED]
                 odo mustard, yellow, tan, green-yellow [YEL-LOW]

       Discussion The color system of Ibo is diagrammed in Figure 13c of the text.

•

Language Pukapuka (Stage IIIb)
Linguistic class Austronesian, East Polynesian
Area Polynesia (Pukapuka, Danger Island)
Source Beaglehole and Beaglehole (1938).
Basic color terms *kena* white [WHITE]
           uli black [BLACK]
           kula red [RED]
           yengayenga ~ *yenga* blue or yellow or a mix-
           ture of these two colors [YELLOW]

Discussion The authors' impression that *yengayenga* ~ *yenga* includes blue is apparently based on the following observation: "Informants found it impossible to compare exactly any of the adjectives with European colors, though perhaps a deeper investigation may establish a few exact correspondences. Informants were unable to agree upon the color name for a yellow pencil, some believing the color to be *yenga,* others, *lenga,* a Rarotongan word meaning blue" (1938:356). That Rarotongan has a form *lenga* [leŋa] 'blue' is doubtful for two reasons. First, Rarotongan has no /l/ phoneme (Pawley 1967:264–265). Secondly, Walsh and Biggs (1966) reconstruct Proto-Polynesian *reŋa 'turmeric' with reflexes in nine widely scattered Polynesian languages plus Fijian, while Branstetter (n.d.) reconstructs Proto-Polynesian *reŋareŋa ~ *reŋa 'YELLOW' on the basis of reflexes in ten Polynesian languages. An additional oddity is that the phoneme represented by the Beagelholes as /y/, phonetically a palatalized, interdental spirant, is clearly the Pukapukan reflex of Proto-Polynesian*/ s/, rather than* /r/ or* / l /.

Perhaps the entire issue is best elucidated by the authors themselves: "We spent about seven and one half months on Pukapuka. . . . Informants could speak much Rarotongan but required the use of Pukapuka when discussing language. . . . Our interpreters could speak only the Rarotongan dialect. Thus a great deal of explanation between informants and interpreters was necessary before the final English version could be presented to us" (Beaglehole and Beaglehole 1938:4–5).

●

Language   Tongan (Stage IIIb)
Linguistic class   Austronesian, Tongic
Area   Polynesia
Source   Beaglehole (1939)
Basic color terms   *hinahina* cream or white [WHITE]
                uliuli black [BLACK]
                kula red [RED]
                enga yellow [YELLOW]

Discussion The author states: "There is no specific colour-name for blue and possibly none for green either" (1939:171).

•

Language   Urhobo (Sobo) (Stage IIIb)
Linguistic class   Congo-Kordofanian, Niger-Congo, Kwa
Area   Africa (Nigeria, Delta region)
Source   Goldberg (n.d.)
Basic color terms   *ɔfuafu* dirty white [WHITE]
                ɔbyibi dark grey, black, grey [BLACK]
                ɔBaBare red, crimson, mud red [RED]
                ɔdo dark tan, mustard, yellow, tan, yellow-grey-tan, greenish-yellow [YELLOW]

Discussion See § 2.3.3.

§ 3.4 Languages exhibiting Stage IV terminology

We have data on eighteen languages which show Stage IV color lexicons. They are:

1. Western Apache (United States)
2. Batak (Sumatra)
3. !Kung Bushman (Africa)
4. Chinook Jargon (United States and Canada)
5. Daza (Nigeria)
6. Eskimo (Canada)
7. Hopi (United States)
8. Ixcatec (Mexico)

9. Mazatec	(Mexico)
10. Navaho	(United States)
11. Paez	(Colombia)
12. Papago	(United States)
13. Shona	(Rhodesia)
14. Sierra Popoluca	(Mexico)
15. Songhai	(Mali)
16. Tarascan	(Mexico)
17. Tzeltal	(Mexico)
18. Tzotzil	(Mexico)

Included among these are three languages—Western Apache, Hopi and Papago—whose classification as Stage IV is problematical.

•

Language Western Apache (Problematical Stage IV)
Linguistic class Na-Dene, Athapascan, Apachean
Area United States (Southwest)
Source K. Basso (personal communication)
Basic color terms *łikai* white [WHITE]
diłhił black [BLACK]
nchi red [RED]
dukliž green, blue [GREEN]
łitsugi yellow [YELLOW]
łibaha brown [BROWN]

Discussion As is pointed out in the discussion of Western Apache in § 2.5, this language constitutes an exception to the partial ordering discussed in the text in that *łibaha* 'brown' appears before *dukliž* 'GREEN' has segmented into green and blue.

•

Language Batak (Toba proper) (Stage IV)
Linguistic class Austronesian, Batak, Toba-Angkola
Area Sumatra (South end of Toba Lake)
Source Bartlett (1929:26–39)
Basic color terms *bontar, bottar* white [WHITE]
birong, agong black [BLACK]
rara, gara, bara red [RED]
rata green, blue [GREEN]

hoenik, koening yellow, orange, brown [YEL-LOW]

Discussion Bartlett (1929) provides an excellent and extended discussion of color nomenclature for several dialects of this language. Van Wijk, who utilizes Bartlett's materials, fails to include the Toba Batak form for 'GREEN' *rata,* giving the false impression that this dialect has only four basic color terms (1959:128). In fact, each of the five Batak dialects discussed (Pardembanan, Upper Koealoe, Habinsaran, Toba proper, and Karo) exhibits Stage IV terminologies when the Dutch and English loans for blue and brown are eliminated.

●

Language !Kung Bushman (Stage IV)
Linguistic class Northern South African Khoisan
Area Africa (Kalihari desert)
Source R. Lee (personal communication)
Basic color terms *!gow* white, grey [WHITE]
žho black [BLACK]
!gã red, rust [RED]
/ouŋ violet, blue, green [GREEN]
gow 'orange, yellow, tan' [YELLOW]

Discussion Lee's materials, obtained recently during an extended field trip, are similar to Bleek's (1956) work on other Bushman dialects. He notes that the !Kung Bushmen have a term for striped or spotted *!hxom,* as well as a generic term for color, ≠ u. Lee's orthography incorporates the following conventions: / dental click, ≠ alveolar click, ! palatal click. *ow* indicates vowel pressing.

●

Language Chinook Jargon (Stage IV)
Linguistic class Pidgin (Chinook, English, French, Nootka, Chehalis)
Area United States and Canada (Northwest Coast)
Source T. Kaufman (personal communication)
Basic color terms *tkʔup* white or light colors [WHITE]

li^ʔeƚ black, dark blue, dark green, brown [BLACK]

pəl red [RED]

ptcəh green [GREEN]

kawakawak yellow, pale green [YELLOW]

Discussion Kaufman indicates that the above appear to be the only basic terms in the language. The remaining forms are terms for colors of horses and borrowed from French, for example, *libló* 'sorrel, chestnut' < Fr. blond; *likrém* 'dun' < Fr. crème; *ligli* 'grey' < Fr. gris; and *sandəri* 'roan' < Fr. cendré.

●

Language Daza (Stage IV)

Linguistic class Nilo-Saharan, Saharan

Area Africa (East Nigeria)

Source Le Coeur (1956:278, 328, 344, 373, 389)

Basic color terms cuo blanc [WHITE]

yasko noir [BLACK]

maaḍo rouge [RED]

zẹdẹ [?] jaune, bleu, vert [GREEN]

mini jaune [YELLOW]

Discussion Le Coeur's description is somewhat unclear. The problem arises in determining the extension of zẹdẹ, and to what extent the orthography he utilizes is correct. Thus, we note:

zedo 'bleu' (cf. vert)

zẹdẹ 'jaune' (but also mini 'jaune')

zeḍe "vert (pour certains informateurs ce mot designe égalemente le jaune clair et parfois le violet) ."

If *mini* is a legitimate term for YELLOW, then this system is Stage IV. If not, then it must be classified as Stage III.

●

Language Eskimo (Stage IV)

Linguistic class American Arctic-Paleosiberian, Eskimo-Aleut

Area Canada
Source N. H. H. Graburn (personal communication)
Basic color terms gakurktak white [WHITE]
            girmitak black [BLACK]
            anpaluktak red [RED]
            tuŋajuktuk green, blue [GREEN]
            guksutak yellow [YELLOW]

Discussion Graburn notes the existence of two additional terms, *swangnak* 'grey' and *kajuk* 'brown', but doubts they should be treated as basic.

•

Language Hopi (Problematical Stage IV)
Linguistic class Aztec-Tanoan, Uto-Aztecan, Shoshonean
Area United States (Southwest)
Source C. F. Voegelin and F. M. Voegelin (1957)
Basic color terms qöcá white [WHITE]
            qŏym black [BLACK]
            palá red [RED]
            sak⁻áp blue, green [GREEN]
            síka yellow (also 'sour') [YELLOW]
            masí grey

Discussion The inclusion of grey is based on: *masíʔösvi* 'grey Mormon tea', from *ʔövi* 'Mormon tea' (a bush) and *masítick⁻* a 'grey earth', from *tick⁻a* 'earth'. This use of *masí* may derive from *masíphi* 'it's greying, getting dark'. However, if grey is shown by further data to be secondary or a descriptive term, Hopi would be a perfect Stage IV system.

•

Language Ixcatec (Stage IV)
Linguistic class Otomanguean, Popolocan, Popoloc
Area Mexico (Oaxaca)
Source Gudschinsky (1956)
Basic color terms ru¹wa¹ white [WHITE]

ti¹ye¹ black [BLACK]
ka²ce³ red [RED]
yu²wa³ green [GREEN]
sa²me² yellow [YELLOW]

Discussion Raised numerals indicate Ixcatec tones.

●

Language Mazatec (Stage IV)
Linguistic class Otomanguean, Popolocan, Mazatecan
Area Mexico (Oaxaca)
Source Gudschinsky (1967:28)
Basic color terms *čoa³* white [WHITE]
hma² black [BLACK]
ni² red, some oranges, some violets [RED]
sa⁴se⁴ blue, blue-greens, blue-violets [GREEN]
si³ne² yellow, yellow-oranges, yellow-greens [YELLOW]

Discussion Gudschinsky notes that "Green and blue are sometimes distinguished by referring to the *sa⁴se⁴* of the sky versus the *sa⁴se⁴* of the grass" (1967:28). Raised numerals indicate Mazatec tones.

●

Language Navaho (Stage IV)
Linguistic class Na-Dene, Athapascan, Apachean
Area United States (Southwest)
Source Franciscan Fathers (1910)
Basic color terms *lagai* white [WHITE]
lidzin black [BLACK]
lichi red [RED]
dotl'ish blue, green [GREEN]
litso yellow [YELLOW]

Discussion The source gives no information about maximal extension of terms.

●

Language Paez (Stage IV)
Linguistic class Macro-Chibchan,   Paezan,   Inter-Andean,
                 Panaquitan
Area South America (Colombia)
Source Cuervo Marquez (1924:49–51)
Basic color terms *chijme* blanco [WHITE]
                 cuch negro [BLACK]
                 beg ojo [RED]
                 sein verde y azul [GREEN]
                 lem amarillo [YELLOW]

Discussion Cuervo Marquez is particularly interested in
the fact that 'green' and 'blue' are designated by a single term
in Paez. In his attempt to explain this observation he suggests
that this group has a less well developed sense of color than do
civilized peoples; that is, "El hecho de tener un mismo nombre
para los dos colores—verde y azul—que son tan inmediatos en
el espectro, indica claramente que por falta de suficiente desar-
rollo en los órganos de la visión, el Paez los percile de idéntica
manera, y que para él verde y azul son un mismo color . . ."
(1924:50). [The fact of having the same name for the two colors—green and blue—that are immediately [adjacent] in the
spectrum, indicates clearly that lacking sufficient development
of the organ of sight, the Paez perceives them in an identical
manner, and that for him green and blue are the same color.]
    Cuervo Marquez goes on to note that this "curious visual
deficiency" (*ibid.*) is also present in several other Indian
groups of Colombia, notably the Guahibos, Tunebos, Sálibas
and Chibchas. The author interprets his results as supporting
the theory of the evolution of the color sense as developed by
Magnus. (He does not cite Geiger.)
    Finally, Cuervo Marquez closes with an intriguing but ex-
treme characterization of the evolution of the color sense hypothesis which reflects the biases of his time. "Si efectivamente
la percepción de los colores se ha obtenido de modo gradual,
el hombre de provenir podrá percibir los colores que como el
ultravioleta son hoy invisibles y cuya existencia sólo conoce-
mos por las propiedades químicas que poseen" (1924:51). [If

in fact the perception of colors has been acquired gradually, man of the future will be able to perceive colors such as ultra-violet which are today invisible and whose existence we know only through the chemical properties which they possess.]

•

Language	Papago (Problematical Stage IV)
Linguistic class	Aztec-Tanoan, Uto-Aztecan, Sonoran
Area	United States (Southwest)
Source	Kenneth Hale (personal communication)
Basic color terms	*s-cuk* black [BLACK]
	s-toha white [WHITE]
	s-wigi red [RED]
	s-ciidagi blue, green [GREEN]
	s-'oam yellow, brown [YELLOW]
	s-koomagi grey

Discussion The presence of grey as a basic term in this otherwise perfect Stage IV system is discussed in § 2.5.

•

Language	Shona (Dialect B) (Stage IV)
Linguistic class	Congo-Kordofanian, Niger-Congo, Benue-Congo
Area	Africa (Rhodesia and/or Mozambique)
Source	Goldberg (n.d.)
Basic color terms	____ [WHITE]
	nema black [BLACK]
	tsuku red, crimson, dull red [RED]
	pfumbu grey-green, green, light blue, dark blue grey, grey, purple blue, purple grey, light grey [GREEN]
	ʃɔra yellow, tan [YELLOW]

Discussion Goldberg fails to report a term for WHITE although one undoubtedly exists.

See the discussion of Shona (Dialect A) in § 3.2 for dialect differentiation in Shona.

•

Language Sierra Popoluca (Stage IV)
Linguistic class Penutian, Mixe-Zoque
Area Mexico (Veracruz)
Source M. Foster (personal communication)
Basic color terms *pópoʔ* white [WHITE]
                    yɨk black [BLACK]
                    cábac red [RED]
                    cú·s green, blue [GREEN]
                    púʔuč yellow, orange [YELLOW]

Discussion Foster notes that the term for yellow is also the term for marigold, providing some evidence that it is more recent than the other terms.

•

Language Songhai (Stage IV)
Linguistic class Nilo-Saharan
Area Africa (Mali)
Source Prost (1956:588, 602, 606, 613, 618)
Basic color terms *karey, kwara* blanc [WHITE]
                    bi, bibi noir [BLACK]
                    kyirey, kondon, kyama rouge [RED]
                    firzi, firzanta firza vert, bleu [GREEN]
                    kara, karanta jaune [YELLOW]

Discussion The alternative forms apparently refer to differing shades of the colors cited.

•

Language Tarascan (Stage IV)
Linguistic class unclassified
Area Mexico (Michoacan)
Source M. Foster (personal communications)
Basic color terms *urá-* white [WHITE]
                    tuṛí- black [BLACK]
                    čaṛá- red [RED]
                    šuná- green [GREEN]
                    cipá-n-(pe) yellow [YELLOW]

Discussion Foster indicates that a term for 'blue' *ciránki*, is "aberrant in that it doesn't occur with the adjective *-pe* suffix. Gilberti's sixteenth century dictionary gives *cicipu* for blue. *ciránki* also means 'blue ear of corn' " (Foster, personal communication). The term for 'yellow' is etymologically analyzable *cipa* 'to flower'. Finally, Foster notes that "curiously *cipák'i* means 'spear thrower'."

●

Language	Tzeltal (Stage IV)
Linguistic class	Penutian, Mayan, Tzeltalan
Area	Mexico (Chiapas)
Source	Berlin (n.d.)
Basic color terms	*sak* [WHITE]
	ʔihk' [BLACK]
	cah [RED]
	yaš [GREEN]
	k'an [YELLOW]

Discussion Forty native speakers of Tzeltal were utilized in collecting the experimental data for this Stage IV language. The distribution of color terms is seen in Figure 14 and the system is discussed fully in § 2.3.4. The mapping of Tzeltal is found in Appendix I.

●

Language	Tzotzil (Stage IV)
Linguistic class	Penutian, Mayan, Tzeltalan
Area	Mexico (Chiapas)
Source	Collier (n.d.)
Basic color terms	*sak* white [WHITE]
	ʔik' black [BLACK]
	coh red [RED]
	yoš blue, green [GREEN]
	k'on 'orange, yellow' [YELLOW]

Discussion Collier's work is the first study of color terms utilizing standarized stimuli in a Mayan language. It can be seen that the terms are quite similar to the Tzeltal forms,

Tzotzil's nearest relative in the Mayan family. As stated in the text, each of the twenty-six Mayan languages exhibits Stage IV terminology.

§ 3.5 Languages exhibiting Stage V terminology

Our data show eight languages with Stage V color terms:

1. Bedauye   (Ethiopia)
2. Duhomeen (=Dahomeyan ?) (Africa)
3. Hausa   (Nigeria)
4. Mandarin   (China)
5. Masai   (Sudan)
6. Nupe   (Nigeria)
7. Samal   (Philippines)
8. Plains Tamil   (South India)

●

Language Bedauye (Stage V)
Linguistic class Afro-Asiatic (Northern Chushitic, also called Beja in Greenberg, 1963)
Area Africa (Ethiopia)
Source Reinsch (1895)
Basic color terms *era* white [white]
hadál black, blue [black]
adaro red [RED]
sótay green, brown [green]
asfar yellow [YELLOW]
delíf blue, brown (?) [blue]

●

Language Duhomeen (=Dahomeyan ?) (Stage V)
Linguistic class Congo-Kordofanian, Niger-Congo, Kwa, Ewe
Area Africa (Dahomey)
Source Delafosse (1894)
Basic color terms *wewe* white [white]
wiwi black [black]
veve red [RED]

amamuño green [green]
vovo yellow [YELLOW]
(a) *fefe* blue, violet [blue]

•

Language Hausa (Stage V)
Linguistic class Afro-Asiatic, Chad
Area Africa (Northwestern Nigeria)
Source Robinson (1925:28, 30, 104, 196, 282, 288),
Abraham (1962)
Basic color terms *fări* white [white]
băķi black (very dark blue, very dark green)
[black]
ja red [RED]
algashi green (grass-green, emerald green)
[green]
nawaya yellow [YELLOW]
shuḍi blue [blue]

Discussion The term for yellow is derived from the name
of the shrub *Cochlospermum tinctorium* whose yellow root
produces dye; however, it appears as though the term may be
applied to any yellow item, for example, "*yā haḷiccē su
ṛawayū,* 'God created them yellow'" (1962:815).

'Blue', *shūdā* is derived from *shūdi,* the act of dying blue
(1962:815).

Note: The orthography employed in the list of terms is
Robinson's, whereas the forms cited in the discussion are from
Abraham.

•

Language Mandarin (Stage V)
Linguistic class Sino-Tibetan, Han Chinese
Area China (North China)
Source E. McClure (n.d.)
Madarasz (n.d.)
Basic color terms *pái* white [white]
hēi black [black]

húng red [RED]
lǜ green [green]
húang yellow [YELLOW]
lán blue [blue]

Discussion E. McClure (n.d.) collected data on Mandarin utilizing the standardized stimulus materials. She collected a form for 'grey' *hui* which may be glossed 'ash'. As indicated in § 2.5, several other informants of Mandarin utilized by Madarasz (n.d.) indicate *hui* to be a secondary or tertiary term. Since McClure's informant was discovered to be a native speaker of Taiwanese subsequent to the collection of these data, the problem of the deviant form in this idiolect can probably be dismissed. We have, therefore, classified Mandarin as Stage V, exhibiting only six basic color terms. The mapping of Mandarin is found in Appendix I.

•

Language Masai (Stage V)
Linguistic class Nilo-Saharan, Chari-Nile branch, Eastern Sudanic, Nilotic, Eastern
Area Africa (Sudan)
Source Hinde (1901:49, 57, 66, 74)
Basic color terms *eborr* white [white]
erok black [black]
enyuki red [RED]
ainyori green [green]
hgirro yellow [YELLOW]
mbusth ollonyori blue [blue]

Discussion The term for 'blue' in Masai is complex and might therefore be analyzable. If so, Masai should be treated as Stage IV rather than Stage V.

•

Language Nupe (Stage V)
Linguistic class Congo-Kordofanian, Niger-Congo, Kwa
Area Africa (Nigeria)

Source Banfield and MacIntyre (1915:155, 166, 177,
185, 186)
Basic color terms bókùṇ white [white]
ẓìkò black, dark blue [black]
dzúfú red [RED]
dlígà green [green]
wǫṇjìṇ yellow [YELLOW]
dòfa (light) blue [blue]

Discussion Note that 'dark blue' is included in ẓìkò
'black'. The term dòfa is restricted to light blues.

•

Language Samal (Problematical Stage V)
Linguistic class Austronesian, Philippines
Area Philippines (Mindanao, Sulu)
Source W. Geoghegan (personal communication)
Basic color terms poteʔ white [white]
ʔetom black [black]
peat red [RED]
gadduŋ green [green]
bianiŋ yellow [YELLOW]
bilu blue [blue]
ʔabu grey [grey]

Discussion In western Samal, skin color is referred to as
ʔetom, though for young babies, just born, it is peat-peat 'reddish'. Of Caucasians it is poteʔ, as it is for very light-skinned Fili-
pinos. Sunburned skin is ʔetom. bilu is not a loan; it traces back
to Proto-Austronesian *bi[l]u. (But see the discussions of Javanese, Malay, and Maori in §§ 3.6, 3.7, and 2.4 respectively.) bilu
is usually restricted to manufactured articles of a brilliant blue.
As discussed in § 2.5, Geoghegan reports that ʔabu 'grey' is also
a basic color term, although it is literally 'ash'.

•

Language Plains Tamil (Stage V)
Linguistic class Dravidian, Tamil-Malayalam
Area South India

Source Gardner (1966a)
Basic color terms *veḷḷai* white [white]
karuppu black [black]
sivappu red [RED]
paccai green [green]
manjal yellow [YELLOW]
nīlam blue [blue]

Discussion Plains Tamil has been discussed in §§ 2.3.1 and 2.3.5 and is diagrammed in Figure 15.

§ *3.6 Languages exhibiting Stage VI terminology*

We have found five languages with Stage VI terms. They are:

1. Bari   (Sudan)
2. Javanese   (Sumatra)
3. Malayalam   (India)
4. Nez Perce   (United States)
5. Siwi   (Libya)

●

Language Bari (Stage VI)
Linguistic class Nilo-Saharan, Chari-Nile branch (Eastern Sudanic), Nilotic Eastern
Area Africa (Sudan)
Source Owen (1908:71, 72, 73, 88, 105, 121, 123)
Basic color terms *lo'kwe* white, pure, holy [white]
lurnö black [black]
lo'tor red, reddish [RED]
ló-ngem green [green]
lo'forong yellow [YELLOW]
murye blue [blue]
lo'jere brown [brown]

●

Language Javanese (Stage VI)
Linguistic class Austronesian, Javo-Sumatra
Area Sumatra
Source Bartlett (1929:16)
Basic color terms *poetih* white [white]
irang black [black]

abang red, orange [RED]
idjo green [green]
koening yellow, orange [YELLOW]
biroe, bĕlaoe blue [blue]
tjokolat brown [brown]

Discussion Javanese may be considered a Stage VI system if we include as basic terms the possible loan for 'blue' and the certain loan for 'brown'. On internal evidence, Javanese may reconstruct to Stage IV. Bartlett obtained the above forms from "the coolie class of immigrant Javanese" (1929:16). He goes on to say, "Neither orange nor violet is recognized by a distinct name. Dark brown, indigo and violet-slate are all light (literally, 'unripe') black [although Horne (1961:538) lists a (possibly quite recent) form *wungu* 'purple']. Blue is recognized under the borrowed names *biroe* (Eng.) and *bĕlaoe* (Dutch), but the underlying Indonesian tendency to confuse blue with green is shown by the use of *idjo toewo* (dark green) for a distinctly bluish grey (Paynes' grey) " (*ibid.*). It must be borne in mind, however, that Bartlett's certainty about the borrowed status of *biroe* 'blue' was expressed nine years prior to Dempwolff's (1938:29) reconstruction of Proto-Indonesian, Proto-Austronesian *bi[l]u* 'blue', based in part on the Javanese form *biru* (=*biroe* in Bartlett's Dutch-influenced orthography). On the other hand, Bartlett's certainty of the borrowed status of this form in Javanese might be considered as casting some doubt on Dempwolff's reconstruction.

•

Language Malayalam (Stage VI)
Linguistic class Dravidian, Tamil-Malayalam
Area South India
Source Goodman (1963:9–10)
Basic color terms *vellá* white [white]
kaḍúpɔ black [black]
čuwɔ́ppɔ red, orange, some purple [RED]
paččá green [green]
maṇṇá yellow, orange [YELLOW]
niḷá blue, blue greens [blue]
tavita brown [brown]

Discussion Goodman's glosses indicate clearly the fact that RED and YELLOW continue to have rather wide extensions at this stage.

●

Language	Nez Perce (Stage VI)
Linguistic class	Penutian, Sahaptan
Area	United States (Southeast Washington)
Source	H. Aoki (personal communication)
Basic color terms	*cimú·xcimux* white [white]
	x̣ayx̣ayx̣ black [black]
	ʔilp'ilp red [RED]
	x̣éx̣us green [green]
	magsmags yellow, orange [YELLOW]
	ku·skú·s blue [blue]
	suk'uysuk'uy brown [brown]

Discussion Aoki, who has worked among the Nez Perce for several years, indicates etymologies for some of the reduplicated forms. Thus, the term for black is derived from *cimú·x* 'charcoal'; 'red' < *ʔilp* 'red sore, pimple'; 'yellow, orange' < *mags* 'gall'; and 'blue' < *ku·s* 'water'.

●

Language	Siwi (=Siwa ?) (Stage VI)
Linguistic class	Afro-Asiatic, Berber, Zenati
Area	Africa (Libya)
Source	Walker (1921:68–71)
Basic color terms	*amilàl* white [white]
	aztùf black [black]
	azgàhh red [RED]
	ówràrr green [green]
	lasfàrr yellow [YELLOW]
	asmáwéê blue [blue]
	lasmàrr brown [brown]

Discussion The form for 'YELLOW' is very likely borrowed from Arabic, and several of the Siwi terms show suggestive resemblances to the corresponding (Lebanese) Arabic terms given in § 3.7. We have not pursued further the possibilities of Arabic loans in Siwi color terms.

§ 3.7 Languages exhibiting Stage VII terminology

Our data include twenty languages with Stage VII terms. They are:

1.	Arabic	(Lebanon)
2.	Bahasa Indonésia	(Indonesia)
3.	Bulgarian	(Bulgaria)
4.	Cantonese	(China)
5.	Catalan	(Spain)
6.	Dinka	(Sudan)
7.	English	(United States)
8.	Hebrew	(Israel)
9.	Hungarian	(Hungary)
10.	Japanese	(Japan)
11.	Korean	(Korea)
12.	Malay	(Malaya)
13.	Nandi	(Ethiopia)
14.	Russian	(Soviet Union)
15.	Spanish	(Mexico)
16.	Tagalog	(Philippines)
17.	Thai	(Thailand)
18.	Urdu	(India)
19.	Vietnamese	(Vietnam)
20.	Zuni	(United States)

●

Language	Arabic (Lebanese) (Stage VII)
Linguistic class	Afro-Asiatic, Semitic, Southwest Semitic
Area	Lebanon
Source	Kay (n.d.)
Basic color terms	*ʔabiaḍ* white
	ʔaswad black
	ʔaḥmar red
	ʔaxḍar green
	ʔaṣfar yellow
	ʔazraʔ blue

binni brown
lailaki purple
zahir pink
burd?aani orange
rameidi grey

Discussion The term for 'purple' appears to be a Romance loan. The mapping of Arabic is seen in Appendix I.

●

Language Bahasa Indonesia (Stage VII)
Linguistic class Austronesian, Malayan, Malay
Area Indonesia
Source Madarasz (n.d.)
Basic color terms *putih* white
hitam black
mérah red
hidjau green
kuning yellow
biru blue
tjoklat brown
ungu purple
oranje orange
kelabu grey

Discussion The system is unchanged from the Malay (q.v.) on which the Indonesian language is based. See also the discussion in § 2.5. The mapping of Bahasa Indonesia may be seen in Appendix I.

●

Language Bulgarian (Stage VII)
Linguistic class Indo-European, South Slavic
Area Bulgaria
Source Forman (n.d.)
Basic color terms *bjalo* white
černo black
červeno red

zeleno green
žǝlto yellow
sino blue
kafyavo brown
moravo purple
rozovo pink
oranž orange
sivo grey

Discussion The terms for orange, pink, purple and brown appear to be relatively recent Romance loans. The mapping for Bulgarian is found in Appendix I.

●

Language Cantonese (Problematical Stage VII)
Linguistic class Sino-Tibetan, Han Chinese
Area China
Source Stross (n.d.)
Basic color terms *pāk* white
hɒk black
hung red
ts'eng green
uong yellow
l'ām blue
tsï pink
fūi grey

Discussion As mentioned in § 2.5, Cantonese constitutes a problematic case in our data because it lacks a term for brown but apparently includes terms for grey and pink. On internal evidence, it is likely that Cantonese can be reconstructed as a Stage IV system, *l'ām, tsï,* and *fūi* being eliminated on grounds of analyzability. The mapping for Cantonese is seen in Appendix I.

●

Language Catalan (Stage VII)
Linguistic class Indo-European, Italic, Ibero-Romance

          Area Spain
        Source Corson (n.d.)
Basic color terms *blanc* white
                    negre black
                    vermell red
                    verd green
                    groc yellow
                    blau blue
                    marró brown
                    morat purple
                    gris grey

Discussion Catalan is discussed in § 2.5. Corson's informant insisted that *negre* 'black' was a 'kind-of' *gris* 'grey'. The mapping for Catalan is found in Appendix I.

●

         Language Dinka (Stage VII)
  Linguistic class Nilo-Saharan, Chari-Nile branch (Eastern Sudanic) , Western Nilotic
             Area Africa (Sudan)
           Source Nebel (1948:142, 143, 153, 161, 162, 163, 173)
Basic color terms *yer, mabior* white
                    car, macar black
                    lual, thith-lual red
                    toc green
                    mayen yellow
                    maŋok blue
                    mathiaŋ, mayɛn brown
                    thithlual purple
                    thith-lual pink
                    malɔu grey

Discussion Several ambiguities in Nebel's report make the Dinka classification as Stage VII somewhat suspect. The term *mayɛn* is glossed as 'light brown' by Nebel. Note *mayen* 'yellow'. It is not clear if the contrast ɛ ~ e is actually distinctive. Again, *thithlual, thith-lual* 'purple' and 'pink', respectively, are likely the same forms. Very likely both may be included in 'red', as may be surmised by the term *thith-lual* as an alternative for *lual*.

•

Language English (American) (Stage VII)
Linguistic class Indo-European, Western Germanic
Area United States
Source Berlin and Kay (n.d.)
Basic color terms *black*
white
red
green
yellow
blue
brown
purple
pink
orange
grey

Discussion Glosses are, of course, identical with basic color terms. The mapping of English may be seen in Appendix I, page 119.

•

Language Hebrew (Stage VII)
Linguistic class Afro-Asiatic, Semitic, Northwest Semitic, Canaanite
Area Israel
Source Zaretsky (n.d.)
Basic color terms *lavan* white
shahor black
adom red
yaroq green
tsahov yellow
kahol blue
hum brown

                sagol purple
                varod pink
                katom orange
                afor grey

     Discussion The mapping for Hebrew is found in Appendix I.

●

Language	Hungarian (Stage VII)
Linguistic class	Altaic, Uralic, Ugric
Area	Hungary
Source	Madarasz (n.d.)
Basic color terms	*fejér* white
	fekete black
	piros red$_1$
	vörös red$_2$
	zöld green
	sárga yellow
	kék blue
	barna brown
	lila purple
	rózsaszín pink
	narancs orange
	szürke grey

     Discussion Hungarian is unique in having two basic terms for red (see § 2.3.7). On comparative evidence, *zöld* 'green' and *sárga* 'yellow' could be of Slavic derivation. The terms for brown, purple, pink and orange appear to be borrowings from Indo-European languages. The mapping for Hungarian is found in Appendix I.

●

Language	Japanese (Stage VII)
Linguistic class	Altaic, Japanese-Ryukyuan
Area	Japan
Source	McClure (n.d.)

Basic color terms *shiro* white
kuro black
aka (*iro*) red
midori (*iro*) green
ki (*iro*) yellow
ao blue
cha (*iro*) brown
murasaki (*iro*) purple
momoiro pink
daidai (*iro*) orange
haiiro, nezumiiro grey

Discussion Although synchronically Japanese is a standard Stage VII system, its historical reconstruction presents some
problems which are discussed in §§ 2.4 and 2.5. The mapping
of Japanese may be seen in Appendix I, page 129.

•

Language Korean (Stage VII)
Linguistic class Altaic
Area Korea
Source Madarasz (n.d.)
Basic color terms *hayahta* white
kkamahta black
ppalkahta red
palahta green [GREEN ?]
nolahta yellow
noksayk green
changsayk blue
kalsayk brown
casayk purple
puunhongsayk pink
tungsayk orange
hoysayk grey

Discussion Korean is discussed in the section on internal
reconstruction (§ 2.4). Note here that the five native Korean
terms listed first make this system a perfect Stage IV. The re-

maining terms are in common usage but are all Chinese loan
words. The Korean mapping is found in Appendix I.

•

Language Malay (Stage VII)
Linguistic class Austronesian, Malayan
Area Malaya
Source Bartlett (1929:8–16)
Basic color terms *poetih, putih* white
itam black
merah red
idjo green
koening yellow
biroe blue
tjokolat brown
oengoe, ongo violet [purple]
djinggo orange
kelaboe grey

Discussion This is one of the most fully developed systems outside of the Indo-European group of languages. Bartlett's discussion is especially enlightening. "As tested in a single
district, Batoe Bara, the Malay of common speech has been
found to have eleven [Bartlett, in fact, cites only ten] commonly used color words. Of these, *merah*, red, *djinggo*, light
red or orange, *koening*, yellow, *idjo*, green, and *oengoe*, violet,
are [Common] Indonesian words which cover all but one of
the spectral colors for which we ourselves have words that are
commonly used with fair precision. [*djinggo* is derived from
Javanese *djingga* 'dark red or reddish brown' (Denzel Carr,
personal communication) .] The only marked defect in the terminology is the lack of an indigenous word for blue, which
was originally called *idjo*, the same word as for green (seldom
now among intelligent Malays) , or *itam*, the same word as for
black. Nowadays one of the borrowed words *biroe*, from the
English, or *bĕlaoe* from the Dutch, is used by educated Malays.
The words for neutralized and deeply shaded colors are *kĕla-*

boe, grey, literally ashy, a truly Common Indonesian conception, and *tjokĕlat,* brown, now forced into association with the
word chocolate, introduced from English or Dutch, although
the Indonesians feel in it one of their own word bases, *kolat* or
kĕlat. The words *itam,* black and *poetih,* white, are Common
Indonesian. The former may be used not only for black but
for very dark shades generally, and the latter for any very light
tints" (1929:14–15).

Malay raises some problems with respect to internal reconstruction, for which see §§ 2.4 and 2.5. See also the discussion
of Javanese in § 3.6 for a consideration of the possible English
or Dutch origin of the blue terms; also § 2.4 and Note 14 for
a related problem in Maori.

●

Language	Nandi (Stage VII)
Linguistic class	Nilo-Saharan, Chari-Nile branch (Eastern Sudanic), Southern Nilotic
Area	Africa (Ethiopia)
Source	Hollis (1909)
Basic color terms	*lel* white
	tui black
	pirir red
	nyalil green
	lalelio yellow
	arus blue
	nur brown
	talelio grey

Discussion Nandi is Stage VII if the term for 'grey'
talelio is taken as a basic term. Otherwise, it is Stage VI.

●

Language	Russian (Stage VII)
Linguistic class	Indo-European, East Slavic
Area	Soviet Union
Source	D. Slobin (personal communication)

Basic color terms   *belyy* white
                 chërnyy black
                 krasnyy red
                 zelënyy green
                 zhëltyy yellow
                 siniy dark blue
                 goluboy light blue
                 korichnevyy brown
                 purpurnyy purple
                 rozovyy rose, pink
                 kirpichnyy orange
                 seryy grey

Discussion   Russian is unique because it appears to have two basic terms for blue ('light blue' is apparently a recent addition), different in terms of relative brightness. A similar situation has developed in Hungarian, where two basic terms for red have emerged. If the situation appears verifiable with further research, an additional stage may be postulated. See § 2.3.7 for further discussion.

●

Language   Spanish (Mexican) (Stage VII)
Linguistic class   Indo-European, Italic, Ibero-Romance
Area   Mexico
Source   Stross (n.d.)
Basic color terms   *blanco* white
                 negro black
                 rojo red
                 verde green
                 amarillo yellow
                 azul blue
                 café brown
                 morado purple
                 rosa pink
                 anaranjado orange
                 gris grey

Discussion The mapping for Mexican Spanish is seen in Appendix I.

●

Language Tagalog (Stage VII)
Linguistic class Austronesian, Tagalic
Area Philippines
Source Frake (n.d.)
Basic color terms *putî* white
itim black
pulá red
berde green
diláw yellow
bugháw, asúl blue
kayumanggí brown
lila purple
rosas pink
kulay-abó grey

Discussion Only the terms for 'white', 'black', 'red' and 'yellow' appear as unanalyzable expressions in Tagalog. The remainder are either Spanish loans (that is, 'green', 'blue', 'purple', 'pink') or descriptive (that is, alternative *bugháw* 'blue', *kulay-abó* 'grey'). Nevertheless, Frake's informant responded in such a way as to require including all forms listed as basic color terms.

On the other hand, Aspillera (1956:126) treats Tagalog as a Stage V system:

Terms for colors in Tagalog are quite incomplete. Our language has no equivalents for the colors brown and golden brown. What is usually used for golden brown is *pulá* (red), as in the following everyday expression used in the kitchen: *Piritúsin mo ang isdá hanggáng pumulá;* which is our equivalent to: Fry the fish until golden brown.

For the color of our race and complexion, we use the beautiful word *kayumanggí* (brown) but this word is not applied to anything that is brown. For brown-colored objects we use the descriptive words *kulay kapé* (coffee-colored) or *kulay-tsokoláte* (chocolate-colored) which are both inadequate to describe the real brown color.

The principal colors in Tagalog are:
  puti—white
  itím—black
  pulá—red
  bérde (or *lunti an*) —green
  asúl (or *bugháw*) —blue
  diláw—yellow

Aspillera lists, in addition to these six "principal colors", eighteen secondary color terms under the headings "dark colors", "light colors", "shades", and "other colors". These include *kayumanggí, rosas,* and *kulay-abó.* No mention is made of *lila.* The mapping for Tagalog is seen in Appendix I.

•

Language	Thai (Stage VII)
Linguistic class	Sino-Tibetan, Southwestern Kam-Thai
Area	Thailand
Source	Forman (n.d.)
Basic color terms	*khă·w* white
	dam black
	dɛ·ŋ red
	khĭaw green
	lY̆aŋ yellow
	fá·ʔ blue
	námta·n brown
	múaŋʔ purple
	chomphu· pink
	sàad orange

Discussion Thai is mapped in Appendix I.

•

Language	Urdu (Stage VII)
Linguistic class	Indo-European, Indo-Iranian, Indic, Central Hindi, Western

Area India
Source Zaretsky (n.d.)
Basic color terms *safaid* white
kálá black
lál red
hará green
pílá yellow
nílá blue
bádámi brown
banafshai purple

Discussion Urdu is an early Stage VII having only eight basic terms. Urdu is mapped in Appendix I.

●

Language Vietnamese (Problematical Stage VII)
Linguistic class Vietnamese
Area Vietnam
Source Madarasz (n.d.)
Basic color terms *trắng* white
đen black
đỏ red
xanh green, blue [GREEN]
vàng yellow
nâu brown
tím purple
hồng pink
xám grey

Discussion Vietnamese is problematic because terms for brown, purple, pink, and grey appear while *xanh* 'GREEN' remains a unitary category encompassing blue and green. Vietnamese is mapped in Appendix I.

●

Language Zuni (Stage VII)
Linguistic class Penutian

Area United States (Southwest)
Source Lenneberg and Roberts (1956:24–25)
Basic color terms

klojanna white	*sossona* brown
glinna black	*kle:qlina* purple
shilowa red	*jekk/achonanne* pink
lashena green	*/openchinanne* orange
lhupzlinna yellow	*/okk/ana* grey
lhil lanna blue	

Discussion In 1956, Lenneberg and Roberts conducted the first controlled experiments in cross-cultural color mapping using objective stimulus materials. With the exception of the nine neutral hues, the stimulus array employed by Lenneberg and Roberts is identical to that used in the present study. (Nevertheless, terms for 'black', 'white' and 'grey' were elicited by Lenneberg and Roberts as part of their initial color vocabulary compilation.)

In many respects, this study follows closely the procedures outlined by Lenneberg and Roberts. In their study, Zuni color terminology was obtained from several informants by asking them to recite "all the color words they [could] remember" (1956:20). This eliciting procedure, without the help of stimulus materials, resulted in a list of fifty-two color terms which Lenneberg and Roberts felt were familiar to the majority of Zuni speakers. As was noted earlier, our elicitation procedure differs from theirs in that prior to mapping, we make an effort to eliminate commonly used, but nevertheless secondary color expressions from our corpus.

Mapping of the fifty-two Zuni color terms was accomplished by the use of clear acetate strips placed over the color chips on which the informant was requested to draw "a map on that sheet so as to include all of the color chips subsumed under one name. The informant [was] also asked to mark with an *x* the one color chip which to him seems most typical of the color in question" (1956:20). We have utilized a nearly identical procedure in the present research, except that we have allowed more than one typical chip per category.

The results of Lenneberg and Roberts' mapping procedures indicate that there were color chips included in categories glossed 'red', 'green', 'yellow', 'brown', and 'purple' for Zuni monolinguals for which there was perfect unanimity in naming. It is of interest to note that the Zuni mappings are in perfect agreement with our findings concerning the universal foci of these categories (see Lenneberg and Roberts, 1956:26).

§ 4 SUMMARY OF RESULTS AND SOME SPECULATIONS

Our research to date points to three main conclusions. First, there exist universally for humans eleven basic perceptual color categories, which serve as the psychophysical referents of the eleven or fewer basic color terms in any language. Second, in the history of a given language, encoding of perceptual categories into basic color terms follows a fixed partial order. The two possible temporal orders are:

$$\left.\begin{array}{l}\text{white}\\\text{black}\end{array}\right\} \to \text{red}\to\text{green}\to\text{yellow}\to\text{blue}\to\text{brown}\to \left[\begin{array}{l}\text{purple}\\\text{pink}\\\text{orange}\\\text{grey}\end{array}\right.$$

and

$$\left.\begin{array}{l}\text{white}\\\text{black}\end{array}\right\} \to\text{-red}\to\text{yellow}\to\text{green}\to\text{blue}\to\text{brown}\to \left[\begin{array}{l}\text{purple}\\\text{pink}\\\text{orange}\\\text{grey}\end{array}\right.$$

Third, the overall temporal order is properly considered an evolutionary one; color lexicons with few terms tend to occur in association with relatively simple cultures and simple technologies, while color lexicons with many terms tend to occur in association with complex cultures and complex technologies (to the extent that complexity of culture and technology can be assessed objectively).

The early stages of development of color lexicon show a haunting parallel with the early Jakobson-Halle (1956) theory of phonological development—haunting because although the strength of the analogy is unquestionable, the reason such an analogy should exist at all is far from clear.

Sound and color are both wave phenomena. Hence both may be described in terms of (i) total energy or amplitude; (ii) frequency, or inversely, wavelength; (iii) purity of wavelength, and so on. In particular, total energy corresponds in sound to loudness and in color to brightness; frequency corresponds in sound to pitch and in color to hue; purity corresponds in sound to musicality or "compactness" (as opposed to "diffuseness") and in color to saturation.

The developmental sequence of phonological contrasts of which Jakobson and Halle write is ontogenetic, referring to the development in the infant (and also the sequence of loss in the aphasic). On the other hand, the sequence of color categorization we describe is "phylogenetic"—the "phyla" in this case being cultural rather than biological.

As in the case of color, phonology begins with two categories, rather than one. Jakobson and Halle call this the "labial stage" after the usage of psychopathologists (1956:36). The first utterance of the infant may be rendered /pa/. There is no one-segment utterance. "The diffuse stop [that is, /p/] with its maximal reduction in the energy output offers the closest approach to silence, while the open vowel [that is, /a/] represents the highest energy output of which the human vocal apparatus is capable" (1956:37). The initial contrast is thus one of minimal energy /p/ versus maximal energy /a/. The first stage is paralleled in color categorization with the opposition WHITE, maximum brightness (= maximum energy) versus BLACK, minimum brightness (= minimum energy). The parallel in this and subsequent stages is shown in Figure 18.

At Stage II both sound and color see the introduction of the frequency dimension. "After the appearance of the contrast CV [that is, /pa/], founded upon one attribute of sound, loudness, the utilization of the other basic attribute, pitch, is psychologically inferable. Thus the first tonality opposition is instituted. . . . In /p/ the lower end predominates, while in /t/ the upper end is the stronger one" (1956:38). The advent of the frequency dimension in sound is paralleled by the introduc-

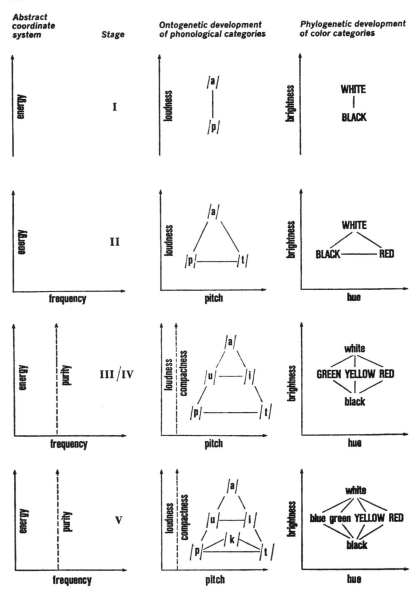

FIGURE 18. PARALLELS IN DEVELOPMENTAL SEQUENCE OF PHONOLOGICAL AND COLOR CATEGORIES.

tion of the hue, RED, in color. Since BLACK continues to name much more of the cool-hued space than WHITE and since RED is focally a low brightness color, BLACK and RED contrast jointly with WHITE on the brightness dimension and with each other in relation to hue.

After Stage II the parallel between speech sounds and color development is less perfect. Nevertheless, we see on either side a progressive splitting of existing categories in terms of either the basic amplitude and frequency dimensions, or dimensions derived from these, for example, purity (that is, uniformity of frequency over the entire wavefront).

Stage III introduces the purity dimension in phonology with the emergence of a diffuse vowel. Color, however, does not appear ever to introduce its purity dimension, saturation, as a *distinctive* feature of basic categories. Rather, it continues distinctions in terms of hue with the emergence of GREEN, which names all cool hues in contrast to RED.[16]

The hypothesized single diffuse vowel soon divides on the acute/grave (frequency) axis, while an additional point on the hue (frequency) dimension is established for color, normally YELLOW. By the end of Stage IV we have the analogous, but not quite isomorphic, structures displayed in the third row of Figure 18. At Stage V the purity or compactness dimension is reapplied to the consonants, establishing /k/, while blue emerges in color. Two fairly stable structures are established which may or may not be elaborated by reapplication of dimensions already employed.

Jakobson and Halle perceived the analogy between sound and color-distinctive oppositions long before the current research was undertaken, and apparently without cognizance of the nineteenth century work on color evolution:

a cautious study of synesthetic associations between phonemic features and color attributes should yield clues to the perceptual aspects of speech sounds. There seems to be a phenomenal affinity between optimal chromaticity (pure red) and vocalic compactness, attenuated chromaticity (yellow-blue) and consonantal diffuseness, attenuated chromaticity (greyed [sic]) and consonantal compactness; moreover between the value axis of colors and the tonality axis of language (1956:33; fn. 29).

Perhaps Jakobson and Halle are right concerning "phenomenal affinities" with regard to synesthetic responses, but our results on the developmental sequence for color would suggest association of the amplitude with amplitude, and frequency with frequency, dimensions rather than the cross-over (amplitude with frequency and *vice versa*) that Jakobson and Halle seem to suggest.

Having already loosely employed an ontogenetic/phylogenetic metaphor in discussing the parallel between the Jakobson-Halle theory of phonological development in the infant and our results concerning the evolution of basic color terms in languages, it is hard to resist the temptation to push the metaphor one step further. The extension is that the same sequences hold in phonological development phylogenetically and in the development of color categorization ontogenetically. With respect to phonology, Jakobson and Halle appear to have in mind a developmental pattern within languages based on the same kind of distributional evidence across languages we find in color nomenclature.

Both the vocalic and the consonantal pattern may subsequently pass from the triangular to the quadrangular pattern by superimposing the distinction between velar and palatal upon the wide vowels and/or upon the consonants. *In the languages of the world,* however, the triangular pattern prevails over the quadrangular for vowels and even more so for consonants—it is the minimum model, both for the vocalic and for the consonantal patterns, with the very rare exceptions when either the vocalic or the consonantal pattern —but never both—is linear. In the rare cases of a linear patterning, the vowels are confined to the feature compact/diffuse and the consonants, almost unfailingly, to the tonality feature. *Thus no language lacks* the oppositions grave/acute and compact/diffuse, whereas any other oppositions may be absent (1956:4, italics added).

About the development of color nomenclature in the child there has been surprisingly little reported research to date, despite the considerable study that has been devoted to the child's development of color perception, color preference, and so on. In fact, we are aware of no study in English on the development in children of mastery of the reference of color words, although some may have escaped our notice. Professor Dan Slobin, however, has called our attention to some Soviet work on the subject, which shows that Russian children tend to acquire control of the meanings of color terms in essentially the same order our results show them to be acquired by languages (Istomina, 1963).

A fundamental problem which remains unsolved is the explanation for the *particular* ordering found. Given that cultural evolutionary factors may explain the gross numerical growth in size of basic color vocabulary, why are terms added in a partially fixed order and why in this particular order? Our essentially linguistic investigations have led, seemingly inescapably, to the conclusion that the eleven basic color categories are pan-human perceptual universals. But we can offer no physical or physiological explanation for the apparently greater perceptual salience of these particular eleven color stimuli, nor can we explain in any satisfying way the relative ordering among them. Existing theories of color perception, both classical and recent, offer several plausible suggestions for parts of the observed pattern, but none will serve as the basis of an adequate explanation.[17]

Perhaps we have here in the domain of semantics a finding analogous to some phenomena recently recorded in the areas of syntax and phonology. Chomsky (1965) and Lenneberg (1967) have argued that the complexities of language structure, together with some known limitations of human neurophysiology, imply that human language cannot be considered simply a manifestation of great general intelligence. Rather it must be recognized as a species-specific ability, ultimately based on species-specific bio-morphological structures. What the particular biological structures underlying particular linguistic functions may be, it is not possible to say at this time in any detail. The study of the biological foundations of the most peculiarly and exclusively human set of behavioral abilities—language—

is just beginning (Lenneberg 1967), but sufficient evidence has already accumulated to show that such connections must exist for the linguistic realms of syntax and phonology. The findings reported here concerning the universality and evolution of basic color lexicon suggest that such connections are also to be found in the realm of semantics.

Appendixes

Appendix I

Terms and mapping for twenty experimentally investigated languages

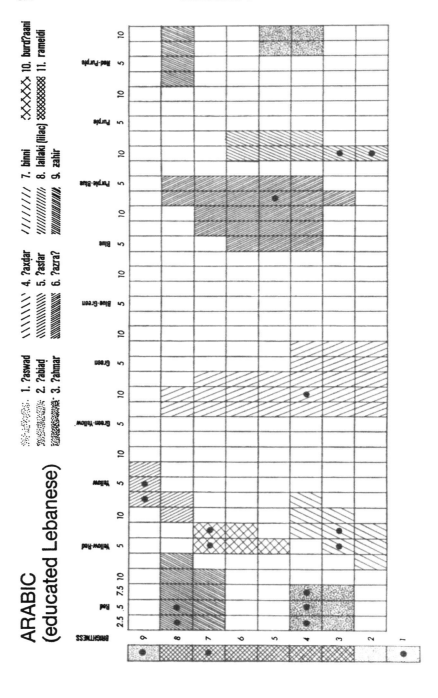

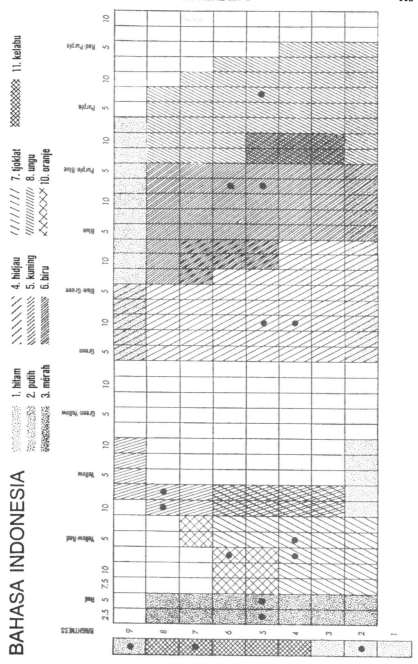

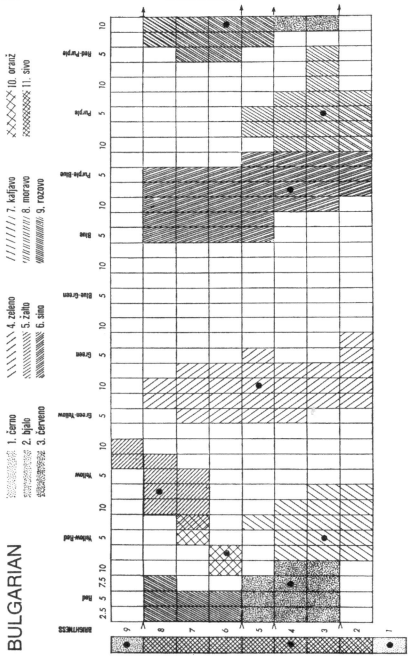

BULGARIAN

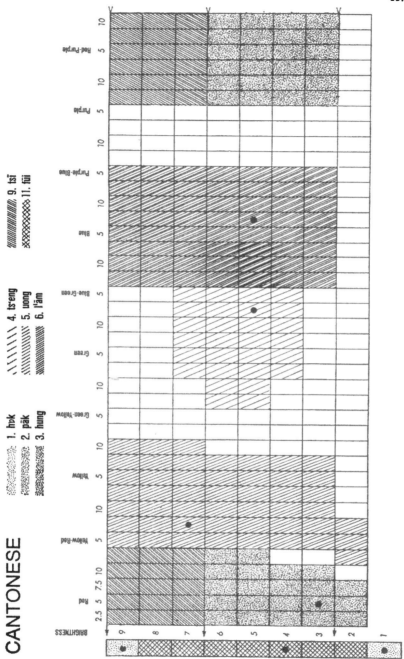

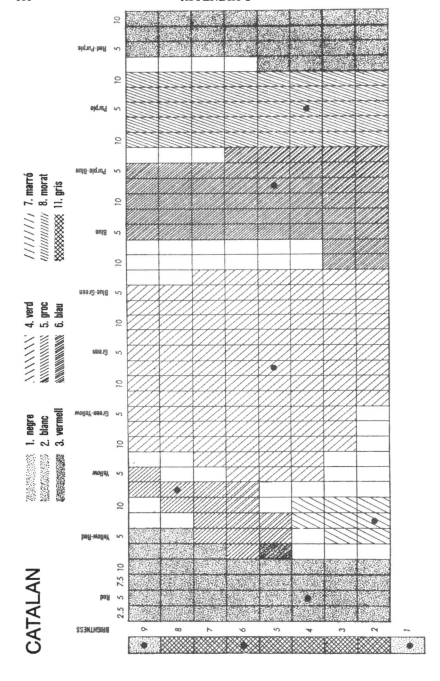

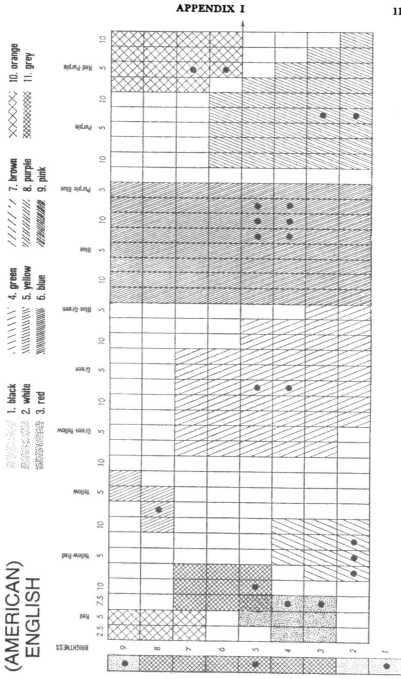

APPENDIX I

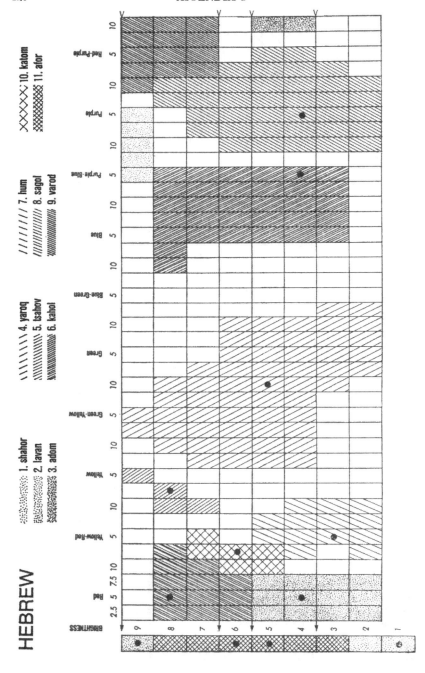

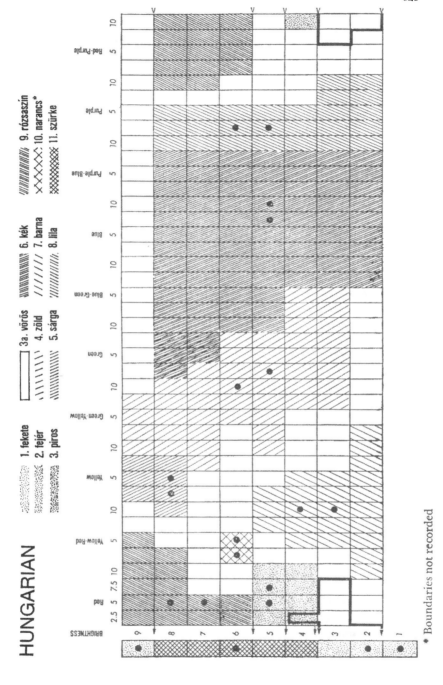

HUNGARIAN

1. fekete   3a. vörös   6. kék   9. rózsaszín
2. fejér   4. zöld   7. barna   10. narancs*
3. piros   5. sárga   8. lila   11. szürke

* Boundaries not recorded

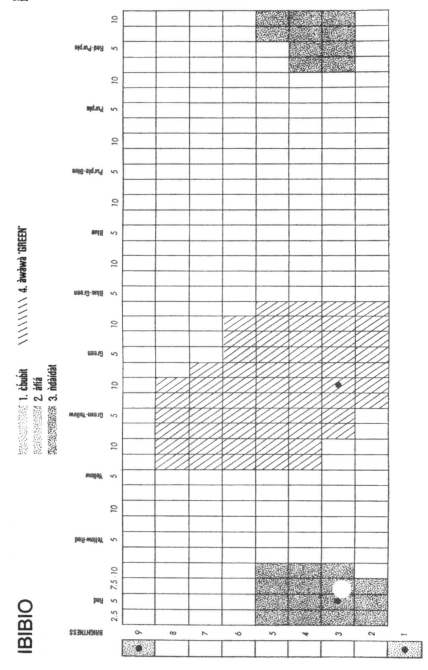

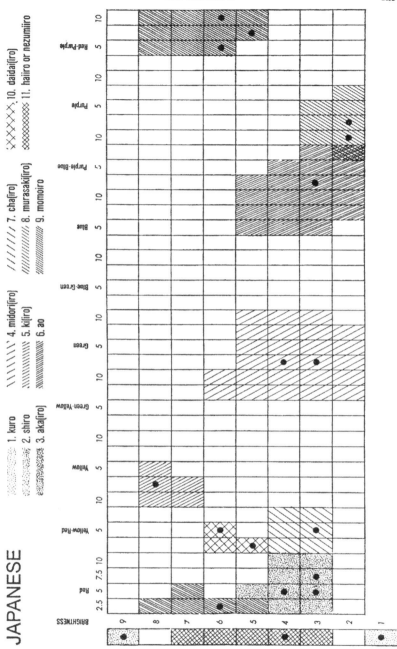

KOREAN

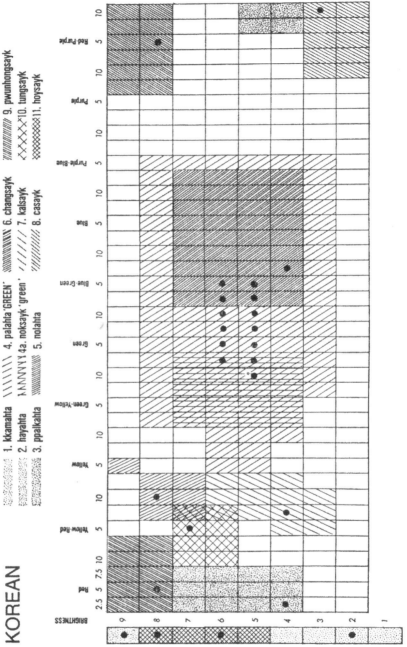

1. kkamahta
2. hayahta
3. ppalkahta
4. palahta 'GREEN'
4a. noksayk 'green'
5. nolahta
6. changsayk
7. kalsayk
8. casayk
9. pwunhongsayk
10. tungsayk
11. hoysayk

* Focus for 4a noksayk 'green'

MANDARIN

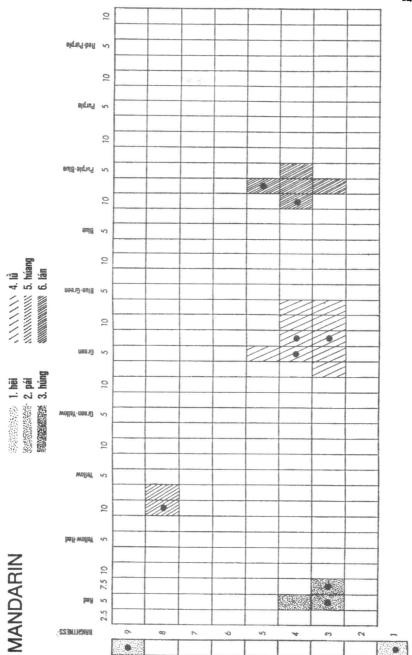

1. hēi
2. pái
3. húng
4. lǜ
5. húang
6. lán

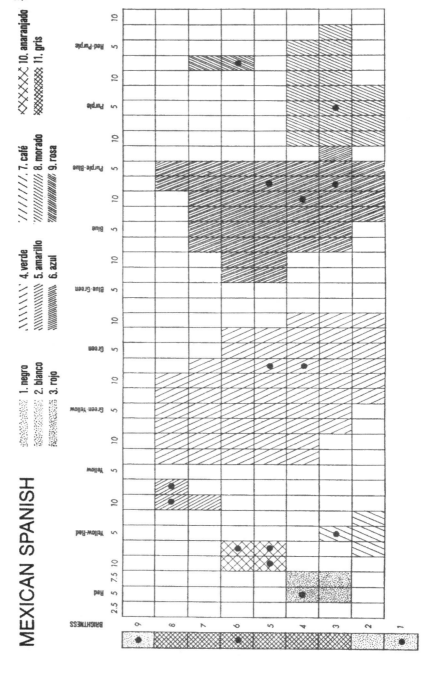

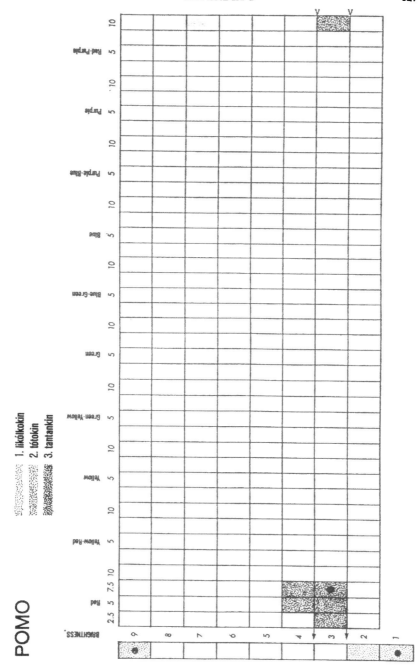

SWAHILI

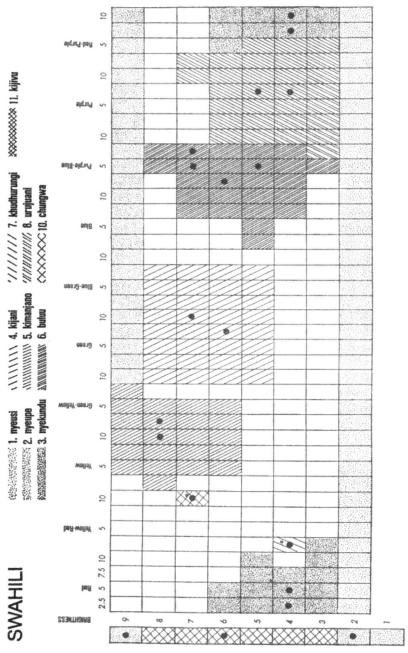

* Boundaries not recorded

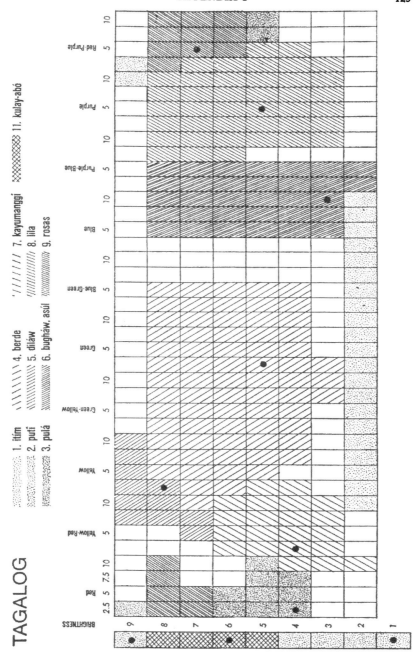

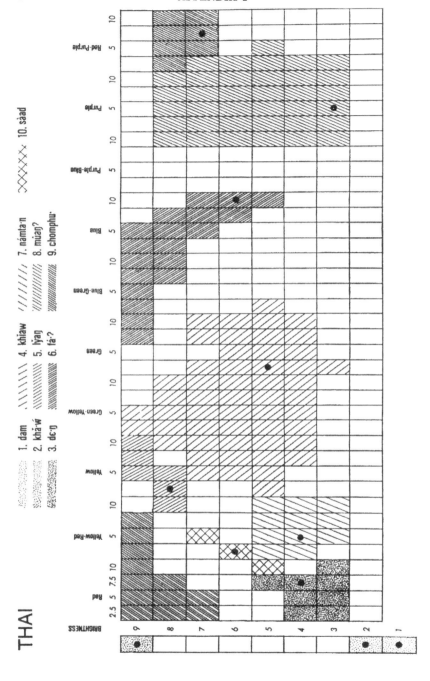

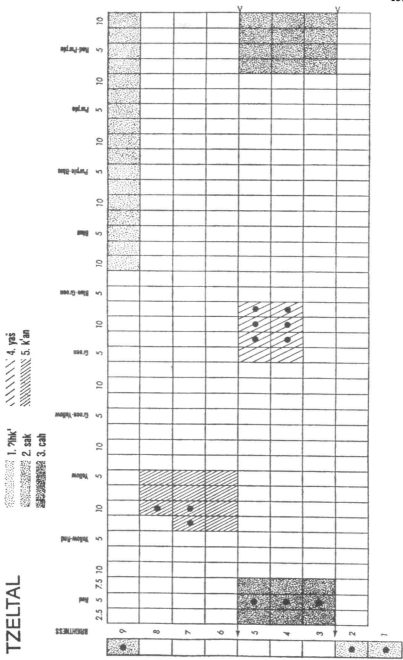

APPENDIX II

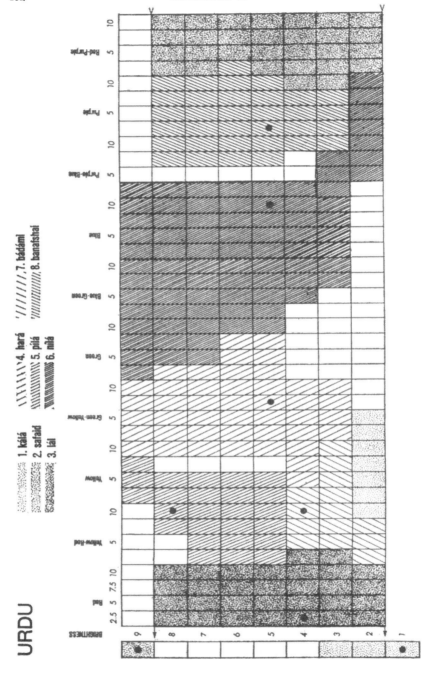

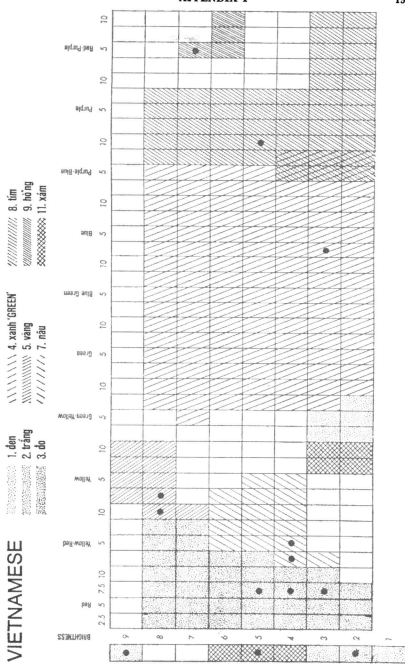

Appendix II

The growth of color vocabulary: one hundred years of theory

The history of science abounds with instances of multiple independent inventions or the rediscovery at a later time of ideas found in an earlier period. Our findings on the evolution of color vocabulary are an example of such rediscovery. After our theory had been developed it became clear that a search of the literature for relevant evidence was essential. We recalled that some psychological testing had been carried out during the Torres Straits expedition led by A. C. Haddon at the turn of the century, and we consulted the reports of that expedition as part of our search for additional data. It was here, in the opening pages of W. H. R. Rivers' section entitled "Colour Vision" (1901a:48), that we first became aware of the long history of the study of the development of color nomenclature.

Much of the early work on this topic is outstanding for its completeness and careful attention to detail, and the problem was treated as a major intellectual issue around the turn of the century. It would seem appropriate, therefore, to review the earlier research, some of which dates back over 100 years, in order to place this study in historical perspective. (An excellent summary from a slightly different point of view is also to be found in Segall, Campbell and Herskovits [1966].)

The earliest work of which we are aware that deals with the evolution of color vocabulary is that of William Gladstone, the Homeric scholar and British political figure. In his *Studies on Homer and the Homeric Age,* Gladstone calls attention to the apparent lack of truly abstract color terms in the writings of Homer (see Gladstone 1858, III: 457–499). His conclusions were based on a comparison of numerous passages referring to color in both the Iliad and the Odyssey. In so doing, he ". . . found such uncertainty and inconsistency in the application of colour names as to lead him to deny to the Greeks of Homeric times any clear notions of color whatever" (Woodworth 1910:325). Gladstone did allow, however, that the Homeric Greeks saw differences in brightness, that is, light and dark. His contention was that these people possessed a less developed ability to perceive color than modern man, ". . . that the organ of color and its impressions were but partially developed among the Greeks of the heroic age" (1858, III:457–499, cited in Woodworth 1910:1).

Gladstone had noticed that color vocabulary in ancient times was poorly developed. It was Lazarus Geiger, however, who first detected a universal sequence in the acquisition of basic color terms. At a meeting of a group of German naturalists in 1867, Geiger opened a lecture with the query "Were the organs of man's senses thousands of years ago in the same condition as now, or can we perhaps prove that at some remote period these organs must have been incapable of some of their present function?" (1880:48). He then set out to demonstrate that man's color sense could not have been as fine as it now is by examining in detail much of the ancient philological materials, including Greek literature, the Vedic hymns, the Zend-Avesta, and other writings.

Geiger concluded that man has become aware of colors in the order in which they appear in the spectrum, starting with the longest wavelengths or, in his terms, "in conformity with the *scheme of the colour-spectrum,* so that, e.g., the sensibility to yellow was awakened before that to green" (1880:52). But he was also aware that a recognition of the neutral colors appears early, and noted that ". . . language . . . does not acknowledge the proposition that black is no colour; it designates it at a very early period as the most decided contrast to red" (ibid.).

Geiger posited at least six periods in the development of color terminology. In the earliest period man recognized but one color linguistically, "when the notions of *black* and *red* coalesce in the vague conception of something coloured" (1880:61).

The contrast of the notions of black and red as the only

recognized hues marked the second period: "The dualism of *black* and *red* stands out . . . as a first and most primitive period of all colour-sense . . . [next to the earliest stage described above]" (1880:61).

The third stage adds yellow as the next color to be perceived. Geiger was of the opinion that man based this tricolor nomenclature on an appreciation of the sensations induced by the night, the dawn, and the sun. There is even some evidence that Geiger considered yellow to include other colors at this stage. Thus, he notes, "even . . . *yellow* is not the pure colour of our spectrum. In the course of centuries the words signifying *yellow* lapse into signification of green" (1880:60).

The color white likewise seems to have been included in red; for example, "in these [Vedic] hymns *white* is scarcely as yet distinguished from *red*" (ibid.).

Geiger suggested that white appears in the fourth stage. "Democritus and the Pythagoreans assumed four fundamental colours, *black, white, red,* and *yellow*. . . . Nay, ancient writers (Cicero, Pliny, and Quintilian) state it as a positive fact that the Greek painters, down to the time of Alexander, employed only these four colours" (1880:58).

Green appears at the fifth stage of color evolution for Geiger. He implied that terms for green had signified yellow at some earlier period.

One of the last colors to evolve is blue. Etymologically, Geiger felt that many terms for blue originally signified green and that an even larger proportion signified black.

Having decided that "colour terms originate according to a definite succession . . ." he resorted to a physiological explanation. He concluded, "It would seem, indeed, that we must assume a gradually and regularly rising sensibility to impressions of colour, analogous to that which renders glaring contrasts of colour so unbearable to a cultivated taste, while the uneducated taste loves them" (1880:61).

In summary, Geiger saw the earliest period of human color perception as simply a vague recognition of undifferentiated color. Next, *black* and *red* are distinguished, then *yellow* (including *greens*), then *white*, then *green* and finally *blue*. The

orderly progression is assumed to derive from a continual re-
finement in man's perceptual ability to distinguish colors.

The first major criticism of the views of Geiger and Gladstone came from Grant Allen (1879). He argued that paucity
of color terms in primitive languages by no means indicates a
lack of development of perceptual abilities. Allen also suggested
that the color terms used by several modern poets, for example,
Swinburne (in his *Poems and Ballads*) and Tennyson (in his
Princess), showed a peculiarly similar statistical distribution
to the color expressions cited by Gladstone and Geiger for
Homer. Thus, red and yellow occurred much more often than
blue and green. Allen felt that Gladstone's arguments on the
vague and imprecise application of color terms in Homer was
invalid for the same could be said of the use of color terms by
modern poets, surely individuals with a "well developed colour
sense." On this point Allen stated, ". . . Mr. Gladstone tells
us that they [the Homeric Greeks] could not have understood
real colours by their apparent colour terms, because the words
are used so loosely. Here, green means green: there, it means
fresh or young. So be it. Has Mr. Gladstone never heard of red
blood, red skies, red brick and red Indians? Do Englishmen
never talk of green old age or Americans of green corn, which
is really pale yellow? Is not red blood confronted with *sangre
azul* and red wine with *petit vin bleu*? . . . Did any man ever
really possess red hair or blue eyes? In short, are not colour
terms always vague, and are they not vaguer in the idealized
language of poetry than anywhere else?" (Allen 1879:267).

Interestingly enough, Allen suggests that one of the major
reasons for the lack of truly abstract color terms in the ancient
literature, as well as among primitive peoples, may have been
that those objects which interested them most (the objects of
"nature") were of such varied hues that single abstract color
designations were in themselves too vague. Allen writes, "In
truth, the primitive man shows his acute colour perceptions
by the accurate manner in which he detects faint undertones
of hues hardly suspected at a first rough glance. How sharp is
the eye which notes that almost imperceptible tinge of greenness in the face of fear, and likens it at once to the full green

of grass? How keen is the sense which catches the slight difference of shade between the black Douglas and the red Douglas, between the O'Connor Dan and the O'Connor Roe! The most insignificant trace of ruddiness in the soil entitled a place to be called *Edom, Erutharai,* or *Rutland;* the merest suspicion of yellow gives us such names as *Xanthos* and *Hoang Ho.* In short, if one object be a little darker than another, the quick-minded savage calls it black; if it have a tiny infusion of blueness he says it is sky-faced" (Allen 1879:272).

Thus, where the broad, abstract color term is lacking, primitive man exhibits a large number of fine and concrete color designations which we would now call secondary color terms, including, in particular, many which reflect productive processes (cf. "sky-faced" above) rather than simple additions to lexicon. (Allen's views are similar to those expressed as a more general principal of naming behavior by Brown [1958:264–287] and by Kaplan [n.d.], the latter in an attempt to explain the partial ordering properties of basic color lexicon reported in this study.)

By 1880 the scholarly world was aware of certain facts relating to the differences in color nomenclature of different languages. First, there was general agreement that earlier stages of European languages and the languages of contemporary primitives contain fewer basic color terms than do the modern European languages. Secondly, there was loose agreement on a characteristic sequence of development, brightness terms coming relatively early, red being the first hue, green always preceding blue, and so on.

On one issue, however, there was no agreement. In fact there did not even exist a clear statement of the problem. Gladstone and Geiger had jumped so naturally to the conclusion that the observed lexical development of color nomenclature must be based on the physiological development of perceptual abilities that they even persuaded their critics to tacitly accept this connection. Thus Allen, in arguing against the assumption of perceptual differences between primitive and civilized peoples, felt constrained to argue against the clear linguistic differences in color nomenclature.

Understanding of the general topic could not grow until it was realized that perceptual abilities and naming behavior may vary independently. This fundamental insight was achieved by an eminent ophthalmologist of Jena, Hugo Magnus, who had already published a short survey of the field entitled *Die Entwichelung des Farbensinnes* (1877). In this work, he devoted himself to providing additional philological data in support of Geiger's evolutionary thesis. He argued convincingly that there had indeed been an evolution of color nomenclature and also supported Geiger in his contention that the ordering must be explained in terms of the development of color perception.

However, by 1880 Magnus realized that increasing complexity of color vocabulary did not necessarily reflect changes in the ability to discriminate between colors. He saw that Geiger could be right about the philological evolution and wrong about the presumed physiological evolution. He decided to examine the two sides of the question independently in a cross-cultural study that in many ways might serve as a model for modern anthropological research. Magnus' goals were, "to determine by direct testing the range and efficiency of the color sense of uncivilized peoples as well as to collect the linguistic connections in which the various applications of the color sense manifested themselves. If we succeeded in carrying through these two points satisfactorily, then simultaneously with the fulfillment of these objectives we could gain a sure insight into the relationship in which the physiological basis [*Moment*] of perception stands to the philological basis [*Moment*] of language formation or vocabulary [*Sprachreichthums*]. For with the help of our investigations, we could certainly determine whether and to what extent the presence or absence of a color-perception must result in the presence or absence of an analogous linguistic expression" (1880:2).

Magnus' materials for his cross-cultural study consisted of a set of ten $7/8''$ × 1-$5/8''$ colored chips. The colors represented were focal white, black, red, green, yellow, blue, brown, purple, orange, and grey; that is, each of the eleven basic categories except pink. The stimulus materials were sent to missionaries, colonial officials, and other persons in many parts of the world accompanied by a set of instructions in German and English which included:

1. a general statement of the problem, including a clear distinction between the philological and physiological issues;

2. a warning that brightness may serve as the basis for lumping hues either in terminology or in perception;

3. an admonition to test a sufficient number of informants to achieve stable responses; and instructions to

4. tabulate male and female respondents separately;

5. test informants once with the full field in view and once separately, one color at a time;

6. obtain the generic word for 'color' if such existed—otherwise note its absence;

7. obtain the native forms in a standard phonetic orthography (English or German depending on the language of the instructions) ; and finally,

8. ascertain whether the terms obtained were derived from the names of objects, from foreign words, or referred to features such as striping, mottling, and speckling, rather than true color.

Magnus obtained information on fifteen North American, one South American, twenty-five African, fifteen Asian, three Australian, and two European groups. His results are enlightening although there are some ambiguities in the report.

Magnus' findings led him to state emphatically that the ability to perceive color is no less developed in primitive peoples —a finding which required a major modification of Geiger's hypothesis. "As regards the range of the color-sense of the primitive peoples tested with our questionnaire, it appears in general to remain within the same bounds as the color sense of the civilized nations. At least, we could not establish a complete lack of the perception of the so-called main colors as a special racial characteristic of any one of the tribes investigated for us. We consider red, yellow, green, and blue as the main representatives of the colors of long and short wavelength; among the tribes we tested not a one lacks the knowledge of any of these 4 colors" (1880:6).

Magnus found considerable differences in the development of the color lexicon in the societies in his sample. He appears to have been most impressed by two aspects of his data: a) the elaboration of secondary color terminology in areas of high cultural interest (note the above cited remarks of Allen in this regard), and b) the lack of precise lexical differentiation among what Magnus referred to as "colors of shorter wave lengths, therefore green and especially blue" (1880:7).

His materials from certain African pastoral groups, especially the Ovaherero of West Africa, show a complex set of secondary color terms for different colorations of livestock but a lack of separate terms for green and blue. Magnus quoted from one of his returned questionnaires:

The results of the investigations of the Ovaherero (or Damara), a herder people living in South-West Africa between 23° and 20° S. Br. are: "Insofar as the color table coincides with the colors of livestock, i.e., of cattle, sheep and goats, there is no difficulty in naming colors. They cannot name colors which do not pertain to livestock, especially blue and green, although they can distinguish the colors from each other and can name them with foreign words if necessary. Because it is not very important for these people to express themselves precisely, they often use their own word for yellow (i.e., the yellow which is the pale yellow of cattle) for green as well as for blue, but upon closer questioning it turns out that it happened *per abusum*. . . . [Among these people] there is no meaningful difference in color sense to be found between the somewhat civilized and the entirely uncivilized. The uncivilized can also distinguish the colors, but can not name green and blue and find it very comical that there should be names for these colors."

Let us recall that the Ovaherero are herders and have innumerable color designations insofar as they refer to markings and coloration of livestock. As all three authorities who conducted the investigation in various places for us assert this uniformly it must surprise us even more that two such characteristic colors as green and blue are handled in such a stepmotherly manner and that even to have specific terms for these colors is declared silly (1880:9–10).

In Magnus' chapter on "the long wave colors, red, orange, and yellow" we find a measure of ambiguity. He started by noting that for a substantial majority of the groups studied, the long wave-length colors, red, orange, and yellow, are most easily "identified" that is, named, with simple color terms. Thus, "In the course of this investigation we have repeatedly pointed out that a difficulty has appeared . . . concerning only the colors of middle and short wavelengths, while for the colors of long wavelengths this is not present. So many tribes mixed green and blue with one another or divided them only very superficially that it seems to indicate a sure regularity. This was never the case for red" (1880:21).

Usually, red was clearly distinguished from yellow, although Magnus noted that "the inhabitants of the Nilgiris, certain African tribes, and others, do not seem to divide sharply between yellow and red under all conditions" (1880:22).

Magnus was struck at once, however, by the fact that orange, also a "long wave" color, was often included in red or yellow. These data should have forced him to modify his hypothesis on the greater codability of long wave-length colors. Instead, he sought to explain the anomaly by arguing that the hue designated 'orange' is a "transitional" color from red to yellow. "The sharp determination and discernment of each transitional color is mainly the role of education, and thus we can attribute the uncertainty which different tribes showed toward orange as well as toward other transitional or mixed colors as solely the product of insufficient practice in color perception capability" (1880:22).

As mentioned above, in all of Magnus' returned questionnaires, the terms for red appeared to be most sharply defined. He noted "the expression fluctuated always within the narrowest limits in so far as it was almost exclusively employed for the color red itself, or for closely related shades such as orange, red-brown, and so forth" (1880:24).

Terms for orange were formed primarily by adjectival modification of the terms for red or yellow, or simply designated by the simple terms for red and yellow.

In Magnus' treatment of yellow he stated that "a not inconsiderable number of the tribes which we investigated had a sharply defined word for yellow" (1880:26). He noted, for example, that in several groups the term for yellow was identical to the word for a certain object exhibiting that color. Thus:

Just as we say "lemon yellow", various tribes (e.g. in west and south Africa, etc.) used the same comparison and called yellow *abonua*, i.e., lemon. An expression similar to our "straw yellow" is found among the natives of Gippsland (Australia) as well. Moreover [the names of] various other fruits which are of an intense yellow coloring or which are used in making yellow dye, [of] gold, and [of] yellow animals such as giraffes, butterflies, etc., are [all] employed for the designation of "yellow" (1880:26).

Several groups in Magnus' sample, not stated specifically by name, lacked a separate term for yellow; some included the hue in red (that is, Stage II) and others, in green (Stage III). Thus:

The Hova in Madagascar were very indecisive in their choice of expression for yellow, and explained that they did not know actually what name to give yellow. A very similar phenomenon was observed among a few black tribes in West Africa. The Témine named yellow *unichéfra*, meaning not black and not white. The instability in the linguistic rendering for yellow, showed itself even more clearly in many tribes who often confused green and yellow. This was now and then the case in Virchow's studies of the Nubians and the Laplanders (as well as among the Ssarts, Bushmen, and some Indian tribes of North America, the Klamath and Creek). This seems to relate to the fact that when certain tribes ascribed to the rainbow only the colors yellow, red and blue, they would include the color green linguistically with yellow. Also the observations which Nachtigal has reported about the perception of color of certain African tribes stress strongly the inclination of those people to unite linguistically yellow with green and also with red. Incidentally, a few tribes among those investigated for us express yellow with the word for red. Some tribes found themselves not at all in possession in their own language of an expression for yellow and had borrowed one from a foreign language. Many Berber tribes, for example, used the Arabic word *açfar* for yellow (1880:17).

In summary, Magnus' materials included some groups with Stage II systems, yellow being included in red, while other groups exhibited a unitary term including yellows and greens. While the data are ambiguous here, it seems likely that these latter groups exhibit a Stage IIIa or IIIb system. It is clear that Magnus' own data did not support his conclusion that yellow always emerges before green.

His interpretation of the short wave-length colors, green and blue, was more consistent. In almost every language investigated, he noted a lack of differentiation between green and blue: "Green and blue are almost always designated with one expression" (1880:31).

Magnus' summary of his findings for green and blue suggests that almost without question the languages investigated exhibited Stage II, III, or IV terminologies. Thus, he noted that two alternative classifications of green and blue were discovered. In the first case, "all identifications were lacking for short wave length colors and the expressions for black or grey [sic] are substituted" (1880:30). This is characteristic of Stage II systems, where mid-spectral hues are still included in BLACK and WHITE, mostly the former. In the second case, "a more or less sharply defined expression for green exists, yet such an expression is lacking for blue" (1880:30). This would indicate Stage IIIa or Stage IV systems as we have described them earlier.

Magnus concluded his study with a summary of ten basic points:

1. All primitive peoples investigated possess a color-sense which in general agrees with that of the civilized nations in its limits. It appears that a variation can exist within these limits. . . .

2. Color perception and color identification do not coincide. Because of the lack of the latter, one may not conclude lack of the former.

3. Color perception and color identification are peculiarly dispro-portionate as concerns very many primitive peoples in that a well developed perception is accompanied by a greatly stunted color terminology.

4. If an inadequate color terminology is present, strikingly often it shows a regular form.

5. Linguistic expressions for long wave colors are always much more sharply defined than those for short wave colors.

6. The linguistic expression for red is the most clearly developed, then follows that for yellow, then that for green and finally that for blue.

7. Confusion of linguistic expressions [for colors] with each other occurs mostly in a manner that linguistically unites neighboring colors of the spectrum, i.e., red with orange or yellow, yellow with green, green with blue, blue with violet. An irregular mixing such that e.g. red and blue are connected linguistically could be demon-strated only very rarely in our investigation [more likely, never]. In any case, the general condition is that of linguistic unification [only] of spectrally neighboring colors.

8. The most usual mixing is that of green with blue. This finding is also confirmed by many other researchers.

9. Color terminology can be so little developed that the long wave colors are all put under the linguistic expression for red and the short wave colors under that for dark [that is, BLACK].

10. Even in more highly developed color terminologies it often oc-curs that the colors of shorter wavelength are united with the lin-guistic concept of dark or indefinite. Blue and violet (and even green) are designated as black or grey (1880:34–35).

Magnus' work is the most comprehensive and conclusive of his time. His only major finding that requires revision now is his conclusion that yellow always appears before green. This is not justified by his own data. One is tempted to speculate that Magnus, as Geiger before him, was able to overlook this fact because of the attractiveness of maintaining a simple theory which strictly ties "primacy" of a color category to magnitude of dominant wavelength. It was not until Rivers' work, some twenty years later, that comparable research was carried out.

At the turn of the nineteenth century, the whole issue of the evolution of color sense in man was reopened by Rivers, who was well aware of the controversy in the late 1880's and offered an excellent review of the literature (see 1901a, 1901b). Rivers felt that an objective evaluation of the nomenclature-perception problem could be definitively achieved only by modern experimental methods. He employed many of these methods with native peoples during the Cambridge University expedition to the Torres Straits (1898–1900).

Rivers' material from several groups has been discussed above. It is of interest here to re-examine Rivers' own evaluation of his data, as in some respects it is different from our own.

In a summary of his research written for a general scientific audience (1901b), Rivers claims to have discovered several groups which "showed different stages in the evolution deduced by Geiger from ancient writings" (1901b:46).

The earliest stage discussed is the Australian tribe from the Seven Rivers district of Queensland, an example of a Stage II system (see §§ 2.3.2 and 3.2). This group exhibits three color terms, *manara* for 'black', 'blue', 'indigo', and 'violet', *yŏpa* or *wăpŏk* for 'white', 'yellow', and 'green', and *ŏti* or *owang* for 'red', 'purple', and 'orange'.

The next stage of evolution is seen in his work on Kiwai Island, at the mouth of the Fly River. This group, according to Rivers, is more advanced than the Seven Rivers people as they have added a term for yellow.

A third, more advanced stage is seen, according to Rivers, in Murray Island, where he reports five commonly used color terms: black, white, red, yellow, and green and a borrowed term for blue.

Finally, on the Island of Mabuiag, he finds definite color terms for black, white, red, yellow, green and blue. Rivers interprets these results as indicating four stages in the evolution of color terminology. In his own words: "In these four languages of Seven Rivers, Kiwai, Murray Island and Mabuiag, we have progressive stages in the evolution of color language; in the lowest there appears only to be a definite term for red apart from white and black; in the next stage there are definite terms for red and yellow, and an indefinite term for green; in the next stage there are definite terms for red, yellow and green, and a term for blue has been borrowed from another language; while in the highest stage there are terms for both green and blue, but these tend to be confused with one another. It is interesting to note that the order in which these four tribes are thus placed on the grounds of the development of their color languages corresponds with the order in which they would be placed on the grounds of their general intellectual and cultural development" (Rivers 1901b:47).

We indicated earlier, in our treatment of Murray Island and the Torres Straits Tribes at Stage I languages, that we feel Rivers' interpretations of these data to be inappropriate. We have shown that most of the terms for these groups, with the exception of BLACK and WHITE, are analyzable and derived by productive affixes often glossed 'appears like' from the names of objects. Again, most of Rivers' reports of the actual sorting tasks with colored wools indicate that contrasts are made primarily in terms of brightness distinctions. For example, on Murray Island, the group representing Rivers' third most advanced group with "definite terms for red, yellow and green" (1901b:47) he earlier reports as follows:

there was a natural tendency to put together all the wools to which the same name was given, thus in Murray Island, Holmgren's green wool was often called kakekakek (white) or pipi (grey), and there was a tendency to place with it other unsaturated wools of any colour to which the same name would be applied. One would often hear a native saying 'kakekakek' to himself as he picked up a colourless wool to place with the green (Rivers 1901a:49).

Inconsistencies like the above in Rivers' work have been pointed out in greater detail by Titchener (1916), who also came to the conclusion that the Torres Straits groups should be interpreted as having solely 'dark' and 'light' color terms. Nevertheless, Rivers' data are of interest from the evolutionary point of view because they raise again the possibility that the paucity of color terms in primitive languages actually "had some definite cause, probably of a physiological nature" (Rivers, 1901b:46), as Gladstone and Geiger had earlier claimed. What particularly intrigued Rivers was his consistent test results throughout his Torres Straits study which showed confusion between blue and green, blue and violet, and blue and black. Rivers did not feel, however, that his results showed conclusively that the natives examined were "blue blind". He did believe his work showed "fairly conclusively that they have a certain degree of insensitiveness to this colour, as compared with a European. We have, in fact, a case in which deficiency in color language is associated with a corresponding defect in colour sense" (1901b:52). In the light of modern knowledge, however, one suspects that what Rivers took to be informants' confusion in perception of blue was in fact the result of his inability to effectively communicate, through interpreters, the distinction between the perceptual and naming tasks. One may further conjecture that Magnus' earlier work was less likely to suffer from this error, since most of the data were collected by regular residents of the native areas. Many of these persons must have been conversant with the native language, and those who were not were more likely to have had considerable experience with their interpreter and a closer acquaintance with their informants than was possible for Rivers in his rapid survey.

The physiological explanation that Rivers eventually suggested as potentially responsible is the alleged fact that the "retina of the Papuan is more strongly pigmented than that of the European" (*Ibid.*). As a consequence, he concluded, blues and greens would be strongly absorbed, resulting in a corresponding insensitiveness to these colors. This explanation is almost certainly wrong, despite the considerable ingenuity it displays.

In summary, Rivers' work led him to support strongly the hypothesis of the evolution of color vocabulary and, in opposition to the views of Magnus and Allen, to reopen the question that primitive peoples perceive color differently than do

more advanced civilizations. Subsequent work on color discrimination abilities among primitives shows no deficiency
compared with civilized peoples. It is even argued by Post
(1962) that primitives have, on the average, slightly better
general visual acuity than industrialized peoples.

Rivers' work was the last attempt to discuss the evolution of
color nomenclature until the present study nearly seventy
years later. A concern with evolutionary schemes fell into
scientific disrepute in American ethnology and linguistics during the first half of this century, due primarily to the extreme
cultural relativism of Franz Boas and his students. Thus, the
ethnographic and comparative work on color nomenclature of
the 1950's was carried out within the framework of the linguistic relativity hypothesis, as discussed in § 1. We cannot here
review all of this work but should mention the research of
Lenneberg and Roberts (1956), Ray (1952, 1953), Conklin
(1955), and, in a somewhat different vein, van Wijk (1959).
Van Wijk's work is less well-known than the others, and we
deal with it briefly below.

Van Wijk is concerned with the discrepancies in the structure of color lexicons in the languages of the world, and at-
tempts to show that these differences are based on the relative
importance of the brightness versus hue dimensions of color
perception. He wishes to show that societies near the equator
have color lexicons which focus primarily on the brightness
dimension, while societies nearer the poles focus predominantly
on hue. In van Wijk's words "it is striking that the brightness
terms occur in the regions close to the equator . . . it is in
these regions that the average intensity of light is greatest. The
average intensity decreases as one reaches the higher latitudes.
Peoples living in the higher latitudes generally use a color (i.e.,
hue) nomenclature, peoples living in the tropics roughly speaking have brightness nomenclatures, as far as we can judge from
the available data. These circumstances lead us to the hypothesis
that optological characteristics of perceptions of light are originally conditioned by the properties of the light, in such a
manner that an optological system with specific brightness
terms is formed where the intensity of light is greatest, and an

optological system with specific colour terms is formed where the intensity of light is significantly less and the wavelength of the light (i.e., hue) is of correspondingly greater importance" (1959:131).

Interesting as van Wijk's thesis may be, it leaves much to be desired as an explanation of the pattern described in the present essay. One of the most serious problems with his treatment is the failure to report terms for neutral hues in languages which are supposed to be examples of terminologies based on hue considerations. Certainly, in the light of the data reported here, these languages must possess terms which reflect, at least, the contrasts in brightness marked by the categories BLACK and WHITE.

A more refined version of van Wijk's thesis might characterize tropical systems as "brightness dominated" and temperate systems as "brightness plus hue dominated". Such a reformulation would bring the theory into conformity with the facts as a rough correlational statement. Still the correlation would be far from perfect, and the explanation in terms of geographical differences in the mean intensity of sunlight insufficient. The major point missed by van Wijk is that brightness is a major dimension of contrast in *all* color systems. As a color system introduces hue contrasts, the importance of brightness does not diminish—the system simply becomes more complex. For example, the relatively late foci brown, pink and grey are absent from just those tropical terminologies van Wijk wishes to characterize by brightness contrasts. At the time of introduction of these terms, foci of virtually identical hue are already present in the lexicon: respectively, yellow, red, black/white.

In sum, van Wijk found a rough correlation between tropical location and absence of hue terms. He interprets this correlation as representing a direct causal relation: tropical light produces "brightness nomenclatures." A more refined interpretation is the following: (1) brightness terms are the first to appear in *any* language; (2) languages add basic color terms as the peoples who speak them become technologically and culturally more complex; (3) empirically, a disproportionate number of relatively simple cultures are found in the tropics and a disproportionate number of relatively complex cultures are found in temperate areas (for whatever reason) .

The latter explanation is more satisfactory on both empirical and theoretical grounds. First, it provides for a finer correlation. Primitive cultures in temperate areas (for example, North America) tend to have relatively simple, that is, "brightness dominated," color nomenclatures. Complex cultures in tropical areas (for example, Indonesia) tend to have complex "hue dominated" color nomenclatures. Secondly, the latter interpretation, whatever its theoretical lacunae (see § 4) , does not rely on anything so mysterious as an "hypothesis that optological characteristics of perception of light are originally conditioned by the properties of the light" (van Wijk, 1959:3) .

Appendix III

Alphabetical list of languages treated, indicating stage, number of terms, and source

Language	Stage	Number of basic color terms	Source
Apache	IV*	5	Basso (personal communication)
Arabic (Lebanese)	VII	11	Kay (n.d.)
Arawak	II	3	van Wijk (1959)
Arunta	IIIb	4	Spencer and Gillen (1927)
Baganda	II	3	van Wijk (1959)
Bagirmi	IIIb	4	Gaden (1909)
Bahasa Indonesia	VII	10	Madarasz (n.d.)
Bambara	II	3	van Wijk (1959)
Bantu	II	3	Rivers (1901a)
Bari	VI	7	Owen (1908)
Batak (Toba proper)	IV	5	Bartlett (1929)
Bedauye	V	6	Reinesch (1895)
Bisayan	IIIb	4	Kepner (1905)
Bulgarian	VII	11	Forman
Bullom	II	3	Nylander (1814)
Bulu	II	3	von Hagen (1914)
Bushman (!Kung)	IV	5	Lee (personal communication)
Cantonese	VII*	8	Stross (n.d.)
Catalan	VII	9	Corson (n.d.)
Chinook Jargon	IV	9	T. Kaufman (personal communication)

* indicates problematical stage assignment

Language	Stage	Number of basic color terms	Source
Daza	IV	5	Le Coeur (1956)
Dinka	VII	10	Nebel (1948)
Dugum Dani	I	2	Heider (1965)
Duhomeen (Dahomeyan?)	V	6	Delafosse (1894)
Ellice Island (Vaitupu)	IIIb	4	Kennedy (1931)
English	VII	11	Berlin and Kay (n.d.)
Eskimo	IV	5	Graburn (n.d.)
"Fitzroy River"	IIIa	4	Rivers (1901a)
Greek (Homeric)	IIIb	5	Capell (1966)
Hanunóo	IIIa	4	Conklin (1955), van Wijk (1959)
Hausa	V	6	Robinson (1925), Abraham (1962)
Hebrew	VII	11	Zaretsky (n.d.)
Hitigima (Lower Valley)	I	2	Bromley (1967)
Homeric Greek (see Greek)			
Hopi	IV*	5	Voegelin and Voegelin (1957)
Hungarian	VII	12	Madarasz (n.d.)
Ibibio	IIIa	4	E. Kaufman (n.d.)
Ibo	IIIb	4	Goldberg (n.d.)
Ila	IIIa	4	Smith (1907)
Indonesian (see Bahasa Indonesia)			
Ixcatec	IV	5	Gudschinsky (1956)
Jalé	I	2	Koch (personal communication)
Japanese	VII	11	McClure (n.d.)
Javanese	VI	7	Bartlett (1929)

* indicates problematical stage assignment

Language	Stage	Number of basic color terms	Source
Jekri	II	3	Granville and Granville (1898)
Kongo	II	3	Stapleton (1903)
Korean	VII	11	Madarasz (n.d.)
!Kung Bushman (see Bushman)			
Lebanese Arabic (see Arabic)			
Lingala	II	3	Anderson (n.d.)
Lokono? (see Arawak)			
Lower Valley Hiti-gima (see Hitigima)			
Malay	VII	10	Bartlett (1929)
Malayalam	VI	7	Goodman (1963)
Mandarin	V	6	McClure (n.d.) Madarasz (n.d.)
Masai	V	6	Hinde (1901)
Mazatec	IV	5	Gudschinsky (1967)
Mende	IIIa	4	Migeod (1908)
Mexican Spanish (see Spanish)			
Murray Island	I	2	Rivers (1901a)
Nandi	VII	8	Hollis (1909)
Nasioi	II	3	Ogan (personal communication)
Navaho	IV	5	Franciscan Fathers (1910)
Ndembu	II	3	Turner (1966)
Nez Perce	VI	7	Aoki (personal communication)
Ngombe	I	2	Stapleton (1903)
Nupe	V	6	Banfield and MacIntyre (1915)
Paez	IV	5	Cuervo Marquez (1924)
Paliyan	I	2	Gardner (1966a)
Papago	IV*	6	Hale (personal communication)

Language	Stage	Number of basic color terms	Source
Plains Tamil (see Tamil)			
Pomo	II	3	Corson (n.d.)
Poto	II	3	Stapleton (1903)
Poul (= Poular?)	IIIa	4	Faidherbe (1882)
Pukapuka (Danger Island)	IIIb	4	Beaglehole and Beaglehole (1938)
Pyramid (Upper)	I	2	Bromley (1967)
Pyramid-Wodo	I	2	Bromley (1967)
"Queensland"	II	3	Rivers (1901a)
Russian	VII	12	Slobin (personal communication)
Samal	V	6	Geoghegan (personal communication)
Shona (Dialect A)	II	3	Gleason (1961)
Shona (Dialect B)	IV	5	Goldberg (n.d.)
Siamese (see Thai)			
Sierra Popoluca	IV	5	Foster (personal communication)
Siwi (= Siwa?)	VI	7	Walker (1921)
Sobo (see Urhobo)			
Somali	IIIa	4	Kirk (1905) de Larajasse (1897)
Songhai	IV	5	Prost (1956)
Spanish (Mexican)	VII	11	Stross (n.d.)
Swahili	II	3	Stapleton (1903), Madarasz (n.d.), van Wijk (1959)
Tagalog	VII	10	Frake (n.d.)
Tamil (Plains)	V	6	Gardner (1966a)
Tana Island	IIIa	4	Rivers (1901a)
Tarascan	IV	5	Foster (personal communication)
Thai	VII	10	Forman (n.d.)
Tiv	II	3	Bohannan (1963)
Toda	II	3	Rivers (1905)

Language	Stage	Number of basic color terms	Source
Tonga (Africa)	II	3	Colson (personal communication)
Tongan (Polynesia)	IIIb	4	Beaglehole (1939)
"Torres Straits Tribes"	I	2	Rivers (1901a)
Tshi	II	3	Rivers (1901a)
Tzeltal	IV	5	Berlin (n.d.)
Tzotzil	IV	5	Collier (n.d.)
Upper Pyramid (see Pyramid)			
Urdu	VII	8	Zaretsky (n.d.)
Urhobo	IIIb	4	Goldberg (n.d.)
Vaitupu (see Ellice Island)			
Vietnamese	VII*	9	Madarasz (n.d.)
Western Apache (see Apache)			
Yibir	II	3	Kirk (1905)
Zuni	VII	11	Lenneberg and Roberts (1956)

* indicates problematical stage assignment

Appendix IV

Standard authorities for the orthographies of cited languages

LEBANESE ARABIC
Doumani, Osama A.
(personal communication)

BAHASA INDONESIA
Wojowasito, S., W. J. S. Poerwadaminta, and S. A. Gaastra
1956   Kamus Bahasa Inggeris-Indonesia. W. Versluys N. V. Amsterdam.

BULGARIAN
Mincoff, M. (ed.)
1966   English-Bulgarian Dictionary. Publishing House of the Bulgarian Academy of Sciences. Sofia.
Transliteration system used is that of the Slavic and East-European Journal.

CANTONESE
Karlgren, Bernhard
1966   Analytic Dictionary of Chinese and Sino-Japanese. Paragon Book Reprint Corporation. New York.

CATALAN
Vallès, E.
1962   Pal. las Diccionari Català-Castellà-Francès. Editorial Pal. las, S. A. Barcelona.

HEBREW
Shachter, Haim
1963   The New Concise English-Hebrew Dictionary. Achiasaf Publishing House Ltd. Jerusalem.

HUNGARIAN
Bizonfy, Franz de Paula
1938   English-Hungarian Dictionary. Szabadság Hungarian Daily. Cleveland.

JAPANESE

Yoshitaro, Takenobu (ed.)

1942 Kenkysuha's New Japanese-English Dictionary. Kenkyusha. Tokyo.

KOREAN

Martin, Samuel, Yang Ha Lee, and Sung-Un Chang

1967 A Korean-English Dictionary. Yale University Press. New Haven.

MANDARIN

Mathews, R. H.

1960 Mathews' Chinese-English Dictionary. Harvard University Press. Cambridge.

SPANISH

Castillo, Carlos, and Otto F. Bond

1961 The University of Chicago Spanish-English, English-Spanish Dictionary. Washington Square Press, Inc., New York.

SWAHILI

Perrott, D. V.

1965 The E. U. P. Concise Swahili and English Dictionary. The English Universities Press Ltd., London.

Seidel

1902 Suahili-Worterbuch. Julius Groos. Heidelberg.

TAGALOG

Aldave-Yap, Fe Z. and Bienvenido V. Reyes

1961 Pilipino-English English-Pilipino Dictionary. Phoenix Publishing House. Quezon City.

THAI

Haas, Mary R.

1945 Special Dictionary of the Thai Language. University of California, Berkeley.

URDU

1963 The Student's Practical Dictionary (Urdu-English). Ram Narain Lal Beni Madho. Allahabad.

VIETNAMESE

Lê-bá-khanh and Lê-bá-kông

1955 Standard Pronouncing Vietnamese-English Dictionary. Frederick Ungar Publishing Co., New York.

Notes

1. Verne Ray claims "there is no such thing as a natural division of the spectrum. Each culture has taken the spectral continuum and has divided it upon a basis which is quite arbitrary" (1952:252). In what is perhaps the most influential of standard linguistics texts in the United States, H. A. Gleason notes, "There is a continuous gradation of color from one end of the spectrum to the other. Yet an American describing it will list the hues as red, orange, yellow, green, blue, purple, or something of the kind. There is nothing inherent either in the spectrum or the human perception of it which would compel its division in this way" (1961:4). A popular text in social anthropology puts the matter thus:

Language (or art) is the mold into which perception must be fitted if it is to be communicated. Any single language imprints its own 'genius' on the message. . . . Probably the most popular, because it is the most vivid, example for describing the cultural categories that the necessity to communicate creates in human perception is to compare the ways in which different peoples cut up color into communicable units. The spectrum is a continuum of light waves, with frequencies that (when measured in length) [sic] increase at a continuous rate. . . . But the way different cultures organize these sensations for communication show some strange differences (Bohannan 1963:35, 36).

Bohannan goes on to exemplify the relativistic position by contrasting Tiv color nomenclature with English (1963:36–37). The Tiv color system is discussed in some detail in § 2.3.2.

Eugene Nida, perhaps the leading American authority on translation, puts the matter thus:

The segmentation of experience by speech symbols is essentially arbitrary. The different sets of words for color in various languages are perhaps the best ready evidence for such essential arbitrariness. For example, in a high percentage of African languages there are only three "color words," corresponding to our *white, black* and *red,* which nevertheless divide up the entire spectrum. In the Tarahumara language of Mexico, there are five basic color words, and here "blue" and "green" are subsumed under a single term (Nida 1959:13, italics in original).

Moreover, the general position of extreme linguistic-cultural relativism and the particular choice of the color domain as the paradigm example is not restricted to linguists and anthropologists. Other students of human behavior have, understandably enough, accepted the myth constructed by linguists and anthropologists, who are presumably most familiar with the

159

data. For example, an experimental social psychologist, addressing a general audience of humanists, has recently based his point of view on the discussion by Gleason cited above:

Our partitioning of the spectrum consists of the arbitrary imposition of a category system upon a continuous physical domain. . . .
The Shona speaker forms a color category from what we call *orange*, *red*, and *purple*, giving them all the same utterly unpronounceable name [sic]. But he also makes a distinction within the band we term *green*. Here we have a clear case of speakers of different languages slicing up the perceptual world differently. And, of course, it is also the case that the kinds of slices one makes are related to the names for the slices available in his language (Krauss 1968:268–9).

The non-existence, *in principle,* of semantic universals has become a dominant article of faith in much of social science. This tenet of the Whorfian tradition is no less firmly believed for being expressed tacitly rather than explicitly.

2. Throughout this discussion, when we speak of color categories in a given lexicon, we refer to the meanings of native lexemes in terms of the three psychophysical dimensions: hue, saturation, and brightness. It has been demonstrated by Conklin (1955) that color lexemes may well include, along with information concerning these particular psychophysical dimensions, other sorts of information, such as succulence versus dessication. Similarly, in Tzeltal, secondary color lexemes indicate not only the features of surface texture but refer as well to features of shape and consistency.

Moreover, it has been argued, to our minds convincingly, that to appreciate the full cultural significance of color words it is necessary to appreciate the full range of meanings, both referential and connotative, and not restrict oneself arbitrarily to hue, saturation, and brightness. We thus make no claim—in fact we specifically deny—that our treatment of the various color terminologies presented here is an ethnographically revealing one.

The data presented in this monograph are admittedly removed from their cultural context; however, we can not accept the stricture offered by some ethnographers that such removal always and necessarily renders data meaningless. The high degree of pattern found in the data is sufficient justification for the process dictating its selection. We thus interpet the pattern found in our results as representing legitimate linguistic and cultural universals. Given the well-known variability in the structure which various lexicons impose on their "field-properties," it appears that our choice of semantic dimensions for cross-linguistic investigation was a fortunate one.

3. The complete set of color chips may be obtained from the Munsell Color Company, 2441 North Calvert Street, Baltimore, Maryland, 21218, U.S.A., at approximately $130.00 per set. Munsell notations for the chips utilized as our stimulus materials may be obtained from the authors on request. A high intensity lamp using a #1133 bulb was employed as a

constant light source. The color temperature at this apparatus is 2900° K
with the lamp operated at the "Lo" position (according to the technical
data sheet of the manufacturer, the Tensor Corporation). This color
temperature corresponds closely to that of I.C.I. Standard Illuminant A.
Illuminant A (2842°K) is considered typical of incandescent illuminants,
which range from about 2600°K to 3100°K. See Kelly, Gibson, and
Nickerson (1943).

4. See the ethnographic methods outlined in Conklin (1962, 1964),
Frake (1962, 1964), Metzger and Williams (1963), Black and Metzger
(1965), Berlin, Breedlove and Raven (1968), and the literature referred
to in these sources.

5. The restriction to *yaš*-normal informants biases the Tzeltal sample
toward homogeneity, and thus in the opposite direction from the point
being made here.

6. The bias, if any, introduced by using languages with varying numbers
of color terms should be toward greater between-language variation, again
in the opposite direction from the observed result.

7. Lounsbury's (1964a, 1964b) work on generation-skewed kinship systems may have a related significance. Although he does not present his
findings within a fully explicit theory of lexical definition, he shows that
recursive rules are involved in specifying the signification of many kinship terms.

8. However, verbal reports of color terminologies, especially those from
the earlier literature, must still be interpreted with care. One frequently
encounters statements such as, "The natives have no words for green and
blue." This statement is ambiguous; it may indicate either a lexicon in
which neither the green nor blue centers have become encoded, or a lexicon in which the green center has been encoded while the blue has not,
with the boundary of the 'green' category very likely including most blues.
Needless to say, such statements can also be given a wide variety of interpretations quite at odds with our scheme. Consequently, reports containing such ambiguities have been excluded from consideration.

There remains a fairly large proportion of the reports in the existing
literature which can, now that we know the universal basic categories, be
unequivocally interpreted. Those reports usually convey the meaning of
color words from exotic languages by means of English, or other European language glosses. Without knowledge of the eleven universal categories, such reports are difficult or impossible to interpret and compare.
(Bohannan's discussion of the Tiv system, quoted in § 2.3.1, is a good example.) Given this knowledge, the vast majority can be assigned a unique
interpretation in terms of objective color measurement.

9. By "loss of a basic color term" we mean here "proceeding from the
state of having some term for a given category to the state of having no
term for that category." We do *not* mean that languages never "lose"
color terms in the sense that, for instance, a native form encoding a given
category is replaced by a foreign form. In Bisayan, a Philippine language,

beldi 'green' (<Spanish *verde*) is no doubt the result of replacement of an earlier Bisayan form rather than the encoding, under Spanish influence, of a previously non-encoded category. See also the discussion of French *bleu* and *blanc* ~ *blanche* in § 2.5.

10. That is, a score at the outside, hence, perhaps no more than a few hundred forms. (Chafe n.d.)

11. We are indebted for this suggestion to R. Kaplan (n.d.)

12. In this and subsequent diagrams, the following conventions are used:
(i) The upper and lower bands of the diagram, nine and one respectively, represent rows of forty chips of neutral hue and brightness (that is, pure white and pure black). The reason for this is that the rectangular color chart used as stimulus may be thought of as a two dimensional projection of the surface of the color solid (which latter has roughly the shape of two fat ice-cream cones joined at the ice cream). The stimulus chart bears approximately the same relation to the color solid as a Mercator projection does to a hollow globe. In particular, just as the North and South Poles are "stretched" in a Mercator projection along the entire length of the upper and lower edges of the map, so in our two dimensional color chart the vertices of the two cones (that is, the pure white and pure black points) are represented by the superior and inferior edges of the chart, or, at least, should theoretically be so represented. In fact, as mentioned above (Figure 1), neutral hues were actually presented to subjects as a separate array. However, in discussing the results it is easier to treat white and black as the upper and lower edges of the hue-brightness chart. (Note that grey is not representable in such a chart.)
(ii) Unstippled areas of all figures containing the name of a category denote the focus of that category.
(iii) Stippled areas indicate presumed maximal extensions of a category.
(iv) Unmarked areas are those whose category affiliations, if any, are in doubt.
The reader's attention is drawn to the fact that WHITE and BLACK are identical to white and black in regard to foci. They differ only in terms of boundaries. This holds true for RED/red, GREEN/green, and YELLOW/yellow, introduced below. Given our convention of referring always to foci in general discussion, whatever holds for white holds for WHITE, and so forth, unless the context clearly indicates that boundaries are at issue.

13. The Tzeltal data were taken in the field from forty informants ranging from Tzeltal monolinguals to Tzeltal-Spanish bilinguals (Berlin, n.d.). While an incandescent illuminant was used as the constant light source for the languages examined in the seminar, sunlight was utilized in collecting the Tzeltal materials because of practical considerations. However, the unpublished work of Michael and Barbara Heiman shows that the type of illuminant—in particular sunlight versus our incandescent illuminant—does not materially affect the results of the mapping task. The only appreciable effect they find is that *direct* sunlight produces greater variability of response because the glare from the acetate overlay increases the general difficulty of the task. (The Tzeltal data were col-

lected in shade.) Their data show that the type of illuminant does not affect the placement of foci in any systematic way. This probably has to do with the greater constancy and stability of color perception in multichrome images versus uniform patches against a neutral background (see Land 1959a, 1959b, Walls 1960, Judd 1960).

Color terminology in Tzotzil, Tzeltal's closest relative, has been studied by George Collier (n.d.). While Collier's methods were not the same as those employed in the research reported here, it is clear from his report that Tzotzil represents Stage IV also. Administration of our experimental procedure to two Tzotzil informants corroborates this finding. The foci of categories in Tzeltal and Tzotzil are almost identical.

14. However, *biru/bilu* in Indonesian languages is not an English loan. Dempwolff (1938:30) reconstructs *bi[l]u‘ 'blue' for Proto-Austronesian. If Maori, in fact, contains a form *puru* 'blue' it is not a reflex of the Proto-Austronesian *bi[l]u‘ and would hence most likely be borrowed from English.

We have not been able to locate Rivers' source, a dictionary of Maori by a Reverend Williams issued in 1892. However, Branstetter's (n.d.) work on reconstruction of Polynesian color-term systems shows no likely candidates for reflexes of *bi[l]u‘ in any Polynesian languages. In fact, few Polynesian languages have terms for 'blue' at all and those instances found are clearly recent. Treagar's (1892) Maori Dictionary lists several glosses for *puru*, none of which is connected with color. *Blue* is not present in the English-Maori section, although *black, white, red, green,* and *yellow* are each listed with several Maori equivalents. Treagar lists William's dictionary (giving a publication date for it of 1871) as one of over 150 sources employed in his own work. Assuming that Williams' 1871 edition contained the entry *puru* 'blue', Treagar must have had good reason to drop the gloss 'blue'.

See the discussion of Javanese and Malay in §§ 3.6 and 3.7 for additional consideration of 'blue' terms in Austronesian languages.

15. We are indebted to Terrence Kaufman for the latter example. See also the discussion of 'loss of a basic color term' in § 2 and note 9.

16. Amplitude, that is, brightness, contrasts reappear in the color sequence at Stage VII.

17. See, for example, Graham (1965), especially chapter 12, and the references cited therein. For a recent review of the literature see De Valois and Abramov (1966).

References Cited

Abraham, R. C.
  1962 Dictionary of the Hausa Language. London. University Press.
Allen, Grant
  1879 The Colour-Sense. London. Trubner and Company.
Anderson, Philip
  n.d. Color Category Systems in some African Languages. Berkeley, Unpublished manuscript.
Aspillera, Paraluman S.
  1956 Basic Tagalog. Manila. Phil-Asian Publishers, Inc.
Banfield, A. W. and J. L. MacIntyre
  1915 A Grammar of the Nupe Language. London. Society for Promoting Christian Knowledge.
Bartlett, H. H.
  1929 Color Nomenclature in Batak and Malay. Papers of the Michigan Academy of Sciences, Arts and Letters. 10:1–52.
Beaglehole, Ernest
  1939 Tongan Color-Vision. Man. 39:170–172.
Beaglehole, E. and P. Beaglehole
  1938 Ethnology of Puka Puka. Honolulu. Bernice P. Bishop Museum Bulletin 150.
Berlin, Brent
  n.d. Tzeltal Color Terminology. Berkeley. Unpublished manuscript.
Berlin, Brent and Paul Kay
  n.d. English Color Terms. Berkeley. Unpublished manuscript.
Berlin, Brent, Dennis E. Breedlove and Peter H. Raven
  1968 Covert Categories and Folk Taxonomies. American Anthropologist. 70:290–299.
Black, Mary and Duane Metzger
  1965 Ethnographic Description and the Study of Law. in The Ethnography of Law. L. Nader (ed.). American Anthropologist. Special publication.
Bleek, Dorothea Frances
  1956 A Bushman Dictionary. New Haven. American Oriental Society.
Bohannan, P.
  1963 Social Anthropology. New York. Holt, Rinehart and Winston.
Branstetter, Katherine
  n.d. A Preliminary Analysis of Polynesian Color Terminology. Berkeley. Unpublished manuscript.
Bromley, M.
  1967 The Linguistic Relationships of Grand Valley Dani: A Lexicostatistical Classification. Oceania. 37:286–308.

Brown, Roger
1958 Words and Things. Glencoe, Ill. The Free Press.
Capell, A.
1966 Studies in Socio-Linguistics. Janua Linguarum. (series minor).
N.R. XLVI. The Hague. Mouton & Company.
Chafe, Wallace
n.d. Explorations in the Theory of Language. Berkeley. Unpublished
manuscript.
Chomsky, Noam
1965 Aspects of the Theory of Syntax. Cambridge. M.I.T. Press.
Collier, George
n.d. Color Categories in Zinacantan. Unpublished honors thesis.
Harvard University.
Conklin, Harold C.
1955 Hanunóo Color Categories. Southwestern Journal of Anthropology. 11:339–344.
1962 Lexicographical Treatment of Folk Taxonomies. International
Journal of American Linguistics. 28:119–141.
1964 Ethnogeneological Method. in W. Goodenough (ed.) Explorations in Cultural Anthropology. New York. McGraw-Hill.
Corson, Christopher
n.d. Seminar paper on color categories. University of California,
Berkeley. Unpublished manuscript.
Cuervo Marquez, Carlos
1924 La percepcion de los colores en algunas tribus indígenas de
Colombia. Proceedings of the International Congress of Ameri-
canists. 20 (1) :49–51.
Delafosse, M.
1894 Manuel Dahoméen. Paris. Ernest Leroux.
De Larajasse, Rev. Fr.
1897 Somali-English and English-Somali Dictionary. London. Kegan,
Paul, Trench, Trubner and Co., Ltd.
De Valois, R. L. and I. Abramov
1966 Color Vision. Annual Review of Psychology. 17:337–362.
Dempwolff, Otto
1938 Vergleichende Lautlehre des Austronesischen Wortschatzes (Part
3). Beiheft aus Zeitschrift für Eingeborenen-Sprachen.
Ervin, Susan M.
1961 Semantic Shift in Bilingualism. American Journal of Psychology. 74:233–241.
Faidherbe, L. L. C.
1882 Grammaire et Vocabulaire de la Langue Poul. Paris. Masonneve
et Libraires.
Forman, Sylvia
n.d. Seminar paper on color categories. University of California,
Berkeley, Unpublished manuscript.
Frake, Charles O.
1962 The Ethnographic Study of Cognitive Systems. in T. Gladwin

and W. D. Sturtevant (ed.). Anthropology of Human Behavior. Washington. The Anthropological Society of Washington.

1964 Notes on Queries in Enthnography. *in* A. K. Romney and R. G. D'Andrade (ed.). Transcultural Studies in Cognition. American Anthropologist. 66:132–145. Special Publication.

n.d. Tagalog Color Terms. Stanford. Unpublished manuscript.

Franciscan Fathers

1910 An Ethnological Dictionary of the Navaho Language. Arizona. Saint Michaels.

Gaden, H.

1909 Essai de la Grammaire de la Langue Baguirmienne. Paris. Ernest Leroux.

Gardner, P. M.

1966a Ethnoscience and Universal Domains: A Culture without Color Categories. Austin. Unpublished manuscript.

1966b Symmetric Respect and Memorate Knowledge: The Structure and Ecology of Individualistic Culture. Southwestern Journal of Anthropology. 22:389–415.

Geiger, Lazarus

1880 Contributions to the History of the Development of the Human Race. London. Tubner and Company.

Gladstone, W. E.

1858 Studies on Homer and the Homeric Age. London. Oxford University Press.

Gleason, H. A.

1961 An Introduction to Descriptive Linguistics. New York. Holt, Rinehart and Winston.

Goeje, C. H. de

1928 The Arawak Language of Guinea. Verhandelingen der Kon. Akad. van Wetenschappen te Amsterdam, Afdeeling Letterkunde. Nieuwe Reeks, Deel XXVIII, no. 2.

Goldberg, J.

n.d. Ibo, Shona and Urhobo Color Terms. Berkeley. Unpublished manuscript.

Goodman, John Stuart

1963 Malayalam Color Categories. Anthropological Linguistics. 5:1–12.

Graham, Clarence H. (ed.).

1965 Vision and Visual Perception. New York. John Wiley and Sons, Inc.

Granville, R. K. and F. N. Granville

1968 Notes on the Jekris, Sobos and Ijos. J.R.A.I. 28:104–126.

Greenberg, J. H.

1963 The Language of Africa. Indiana University Research Center in Anthropology, Folklore and Linguistics. Publication 25.

Gudschinsky, Sarah

1956 The ABC's of Lexicostatistics. Word. 12:175–210.

1967 How to Learn an Unwritten Language. New York. Holt, Rinehart and Winston.

Heider, Karl G.
1965 The Dugum Dani: A Papuan Culture of the West New Guinea Highlands. Harvard University. Unpublished Doctoral Dissertation.
Hinde, Hildegarde
1901 The Masai Language. London. Cambridge University Press.
Hollis, A. C.
1909 The Nandi: Their Language and Folklore. Oxford. Clarendon Press.
Horne, Elinor C.
1961 Beginning Javanese. New Haven and London. Yale University Press.
Istomina, Z. M.
1963 Perception and Naming of Color in Early Childhood. Soviet Psychology and Psychiatry. 1:37–45.
Jakobson, Roman and Morris Halle
1956 Fundamentals of Language. The Hague. Mouton.
Judd, D. B.
1960 Appraisal of Land's Work on Two-Primary Color Projections. Journal of the Optical Society of America. 50:254–268.
Kaplan, Ronald M.
n.d. Towards an Explanation of the Universality and Evolution of Basic Color Terms. University of California, Berkeley. Unpublished term paper.
Kaufman, Elaine
n.d. Ibibio Color Categories. Berkeley. Unpublished manuscript.
Kay, Paul
n.d. Lebanese Arabic Color Terms. Berkeley. Unpublished manuscript.
Kelly, K. L., K. S. Gibson, and D. Nickerson
1943 Tristimulus Specification of the Munsell Book of Color from Spectrophotometric Measurements. Journal of the Optical Society of America. 33,7:355–376.
Kennedy, D. G.
1931 Field Notes on the Culture of Vaitupu, Ellice Island. Memoirs of the Polynesian Society. Vol. 9. New Plymouth, N.Z. Thomas Avery and Sons, Ltd.
Kepner, William A.
1905 Observations on Color Perception among the Bisayans of Leyte Island, P. I. Science. 22:599–683.
Kirchhoff, Albrecht
1883 Die Wissenschaft. Ergebnisse d. Vega expedition Bd. 1 5. 42.
Kirk, J. W. C.
1905 A Grammar of the Somali Language. London. Cambridge University Press
Krauss, Robert M.
1968 Language as a Symbolic Process in Communication. American Scientist. 56, 3:265–278.

Land, E. H.
  1959a Color Vision and the Natural Image. Part I. Proceedings of the National Academy of Sciences. 45:115–129.
  1959b Color Vision and the Natural Image. Part II. Proceedings of the National Academy of Sciences. 45:636–644.

Le Coeur, Charles
  1956 Grammaire et tetes Tada-Daza. Dakar. Mémoires de l'Institut Français D'Afrique Noir. (IFAN).

Lenneberg, Eric H.
  1967 Biological Foundations of Language. New York. John Wiley and Sons.

Lenneberg, Eric H. and John M. Roberts
  1956 The Language of Experience: A Study in Methodology. Memoir 13 of International Journal of American Linguistics.

Lounsbury, Floyd
  1964a A Formal Account of the Crow and Omaha-type Kinship Terminologies. in Explorations in Cultural Anthropology: Essays presented to George Peter Murdock. W. H. Goodenough (ed.), New York. McGraw Hill. pp. 351–393.
  1964b The Structural Analysis of Kinship Semantics. in Proceedings of the Ninth International Congress of Linguistics. (Cambridge, Mass.) The Hague. Mouton. pp. 1073–1093.

Madarasz, Paul
  n.d. Seminar paper on color categories. University of California, Berkeley. Unpublished manuscript.

Magnus, Hugo
  1877 Die geschichtliche Entwickelung des Farbensinnes. Leipzig. Viet.
  1880 Untersuchungen über den Farbensinn der Nâturvölker. Jena. Fraher.

McClure, Erica
  n.d. Seminar paper on color categories. University of California, Berkeley. Unpublished manuscript.

Metzger, Duane, and Gerald D. Williams
  1963 A Formal Ethnographic Analysis of Tenejapa Ladino Weddings. American Anthropologist. 65:1073–1101.

Migeod, Frederick W. H.
  1908 The Mende Language. London. Kegan, Paul, Trench, Trubner and Company, Ltd.

Nebel, P. A.
  1948 Dinka Grammar. Verona. Missioni Africane.

Nida, Eugene A.
  1959 Principles of translation as exemplified by Bible translating. In Reuben A. Brower (ed.). "On Translation." Cambridge. Harvard University Press. pp. 11–31.

Nylander, Gustavus R.
  1814 Grammar and Vocabulary of the Bulom Language. London. Ellerton and Henderson.

Owen, Roger C. R.
  1908 Bari Grammar and Vocabulary. London. J. and E. Bumpus Ltd.

Pawley, Andrew
  1967 The Relationships of Polynesian Outlier Language. Journal of
       the Polynesian Society. 76,3:259–296.
Post, Richard H.
  1962 Population Differences in Vision Acuity. A review with specula-
       tive notes on selection relaxation. Eugenics Quarterly. 9.4:189–
       212.
Prost, André
  1956 La Langue Sonay. Dakar. Mémoires de l'Institut d'Afrique
       Noire. #47.
Rausch, P. J.
  1912 Die Sprache von Südost-Bougainville, Deutsche Salomon-Inseln.
       Anthropos. 7:105–134, 585–616, 964–994.
Ray, Verne F.
  1952 Techniques and Problems in the Study of Human Color Percep-
       tion. Southwestern Journal of Anthropology. 8:251–259.
  1953 Human Color Perception and Behavioral Response. Transactions.
       New York Academy of Sciences. (ser. 2). 16:98–104.
Reinsch
  1895 Worterbuch der Bedauye-sprache. Vienna. Alfred Holden.
Rivers, W. H. R.
  1901a Introduction and Vision. in A. C. Haddon (ed.) Reports on
        the Cambridge Anthropological Expedition to the Torres Straits.
        Vol. II, Physiology and Psychology, part I.
  1901b Primitive Color Vision. Popular Science Monthly. 59:44–58.
  1905 Observations on the Senses of the Todas. British Journal of
       Psychology. I:321.
Robinson, Charles Henry
  1925 Dictionary of the Hausa Language. London. Cambridge Uni-
       versity Press.
Romney, A. Kimball
  1967 Internal Reconstruction of Yuman Kinship Terminology in
       Dell H. Hymes with William E. Bittle (eds.). Studies in South-
       western Ethnolinguistics.The Hague. Paris. Mouton and Com-
       pany. pp. 379–388.
Sapir, Edward
  1916 Time Perspective in Aboriginal American Culture: A Study in
       Method. In David Mandelbaum (ed.), Selected Writings of
       Edward Sapir in Language, Culture and Personality. Berkeley
       and Los Angeles. University of California Press. 1949.
Segall, M. H., D. T. Campbell and M. J. Herskovits
  1966 The Influence of Culture on Visual Perception. Indianapolis.
       Bobbs-Merrill.
Simon, K.
  1951 Colour Vision of Buganda Africans. East African Medical Jour-
       nal. 28:59–75.
Smith, Edwin W.
  1907 A Handbook of the Ila Language. London. Oxford University
       Press.

Spencer, B. and F. J. Gillen
    1927 The Arunta; A Study of a Stone Age People. London. Macmillan
        and Company.
Stapleton, Walter H.
    1903 Comparative Handbook of the Congo Languages. London.
        Baptist Missionary Society Press.
Steager, Peter
    n.d. Seminar paper on color categories. University of California,
        Berkeley. Unpublished manuscript.
Stross, Brian
    n.d. Seminar paper on color categories. University of California,
        Berkeley. Unpublished manuscript.
Titchener, E. B.
    1961 On Ethnological Tests of Sensation and Perception with special
        reference to tests of color vision and tactile discrimination
        described in the reports of the Cambridge anthropological ex-
        pedition to Torres Straits. Proceedings of the American Philo-
        sophical Society. 55:204-236.
Treagar, Edward
    1892 Maori-Polynesian Comparative Dictionary. Christchurch, Wel-
        lington and Dunedin (New Zealand). Whitcombe and Tombs,
        Ltd.
Turner, Victor
    1966 Color Classification in Ndembu Ritual. In Banton (ed.) Anthro-
        pological Approaches to the Study of Religion. Association of
        Social Anthropology Monographs.
van Wijk, H. A. C. W.
    1959 A Cross-cultural Theory of Colour and Brightness Nomencla-
        ture. The Hague. Bijdragen tot de Taal-, Land-, en Volkenkinde
        15. 2:113-137.
von Hagen, Gunther T.
    1914 Lehrbuch der Bulu-sprache. Berlin. Druck and Verlag von Gebr.
        Rodetzki Hofbuchhandlung.
Voegelin, Carl F. and Florence M. Voegelin
    1957 Hopi Domains. Indiana University Publication in Anthropology
        and Linguistics. Memoir #14 of the International Journal of
        American Linguistics.
Walker, W. Seymour
    1921 The Siwi Language. London. Kegan, Paul, Trench, Trubner
        and Company, Ltd.
Walls, G.
    1960 Land! Land! Psychological Bulletin. 57:29-48.
Walsh, D. S. and Bruce Biggs
    1966 Proto-Polynesian Word List I. Te Reo Monographs. Auckland.
        Linguistic Society of New Zealand.
Woodworth, R. S.
    1910 The Puzzle of Color Vocabularies. Psychology Bulletin 7:325-
        334.

Zahan, D.
1951 Les Coleurs Chez les Bambara du Soudan Français. Notes Africaines. 50:53–56.
Zaretsky, Kathleen MacLaren
n.d. Seminar paper on color categories. University of California, Berkeley. Unpublished manuscript.

A Bibliography
of Color Categorization Research,
1970–1990
by Luisa Maffi

The bibliography presented in the following pages is the first comprehensive compilation of the vast literature on color categorization and naming that has appeared in the twenty years since the publication of Berlin and Kay's *Basic Color Terms* (BCT) in 1969, with the addition of a few relevant earlier works not mentioned in BCT. It was originally gathered as part of an extensive critical appraisal of BCT and the post-BCT literature (see Maffi 1990 ms. below).

The references reflect a fairly thorough coverage of the work of anthropologists, linguists, and cognitive psychologists, who have carried out the bulk of research on how humans around the world conceive of, and refer to, colors. No attempt has been made at exhaustive coverage of the importantly related fields of the physiology and psychophysics of color vision, which in the past twenty years alone have yielded a production as abundant as, if not greater than, that of the other three fields together. Only those works in this domain that most directly bear on the recent developments of color categorization theory are mentioned. Likewise, only very partial reference is made to another important body of writing on color: that produced by philosophers, whose interest in the topic has the longest history. An effort has been made to cover not only U.S. but also European sources, most of the latter being in either English or French. In spite of close scrutiny, some relevant works may still have escaped the bibliographic sieve. This is virtually inevitable in a universe of the magnitude and multiformity of color categorization literature.

Among the works listed below, the reader will find, in the first place, the more recent research on color categorization and naming by Berlin and Kay and their collaborators, representing the developments of the original BCT theoretical framework, especially as

173

a consequence of further empirical studies by these and numerous other authors. The largest part of the anthropological and linguistic literature on color is indeed comprised of ethnographic descriptions of color classification systems in individual languages (with the addition of some historical reconstructions of such systems in protolanguages). Many of these, both supporting and questioning BCT, are included in the present bibliography.

Reviews, critiques, and commentaries of BCT are also included, as are a few proposed theoretical alternatives to, or partial modifications of, the BCT framework and its developments. Several pieces address the debated issue of Sapir-Whorfian cultural relativity in color categorization and naming. Others take up the difficult topic of the possible correlations between stage of color lexicon and degree of cultural complexity and technological development, or provide internal evidence on the evolution of color classification systems. The possible ontogenetic and phylogenetic bases of color categorization are also dealt with in a number of works. The physiological and psychophysical literature covers aspects of color vision in humans (adults and infants) and other primates. The cognitive psychological literature provides insights from a cross-cultural psychological point of view, as well as developing central notions such as those of prototype, basic-level category, and salience. Among the many other topics dealt with in the works that follow, it may suffice to further mention intracultural variability, the effects of language and culture contact on color categorization and naming, and the sound symbolic and affective components of color vocabularies.

Only a sample of the richness and complexity of a domain whose relevance, often questioned at the initial stages of development of the theory as "a mere question of ethnographic semantics," can now hardly be denied in its implications for the synchronic and diachronic understanding of human cognition.

Adams, Francis M., and Charles E. Osgood
  1973 A cross-cultural study of the affective meaning of color. *Journal of Cross-cultural Psychology* 4(2):135–156.
Aldrich, Jean Wheelwright
  1976 Anglo-Saxon color words. Santa Barbara, CA: ms.
Allott, R. M.
  1974 Some apparent uniformities between languages in colour-naming. *Language and Speech* 17:377–402.
Aristotle
  1913 *De Coloribus.* T. Lovejoy and E. S. Forster, eds. Oxford: Clarendon Press.
Aulakh, Gurinder S.
  n.d. Color terms and categories in Panjabi. University of California, Berkeley: ms.
Baines, John
  1985 Color terminology and color classification: Ancient Egyptian color terminology and polychromy. *American Anthropologist* 87(2):282–297.
Beare, Aleeza Cerf
  1963 Color-name as a function of wave-length. *The American Journal of Psychology* 76:248–256.
Bender, M. Lionel
  1983 Color term encoding in a special lexical domain: Sudanese Arabic skin colors. *Anthropological Linguistics* 25(1):19–27.
Berlin, Brent
  1970 [1966] A universalist-evolutionary approach in ethnographic semantics. In Fischer (1970), pp. 3–18.
Berlin, Brent
  n.d. Tzeltal color terminology. University of California, Berkeley: ms.
Berlin, Brent, and Elois Ann Berlin
  1975 Aguaruna color categories. *American Ethnologist* 2(1):61–87
Berlin, Brent, Paul Kay, and William R. Merrifield
  1985 Color term evolution: Recent evidence from the World Color Survey. Paper presented at the 84th meeting of the American Anthropological Association, Washington, D.C.
Bolton, Ralph
  1978 Black, white, and red all over: The riddle of color term salience. *Ethnology* 17(3):287–311.
Bolton, Ralph, Anne Curtis, and Lynn L. Thomas
  1980 Nepali color terms: Salience on a listing task. *Journal of the Steward Anthropological Society* 12:309–322.
Bornstein, Marc H.
  1973a The psychophysiological component of cultural difference in color naming and illusion susceptibility. *Behavioral Science Notes* 1:41–101.
Bornstein, Marc H.
  1973b Color vision and color naming: A psychophysiological hypothesis of cultural difference. *Psychological Bulletin* 80(4):257–285.

Bornstein, Marc H.
1975a The influence of visual perception on culture. *American Anthropologist* 77:774–798.
Bornstein, Marc H.
1975b Qualities of color vision in infancy. *Journal of Experimental Child Psychology* 19:401–419.
Bornstein, Marc H.
1978 Considérations sur l'organisation des tonalités chromatiques. In Tornay (1978a), pp. 71–82.
Bornstein, Marc H.
1985 Colour-name versus shape-name learning in young children. *Journal of Child Language* 12(2):387–393.
Bornstein, Marc H., William Kessen, and Sally Weiskopf
1976 The categories of hue in infancy. *Science* 191(4223):201–202.
Boster, James S.
1986 Can individuals recapitulate the evolutionary development of color lexicons? *Ethnology* 25(1):61–74.
Boynton, Robert M.
1979 *Human Color Vision.* New York: Holt, Rinehart and Winston.
Boynton, Robert M.
1988 *Color vision. In Annual Review of Psychology,* pp. 69–100. Palo Alto: Annual Reviews, Inc.
Boynton, Robert M., Robert E. MacLaury, and Keiji Uchikawa
1989 Centroids of color categories compared by two methods. *Color Research and Application* 14(1):6–15.
Boynton, Robert M., and Conrad X. Olson
1987 Locating basic colors in the OSA space. *Color Research and Application* 12:107–123.
Brakel, J. van
n.d. The plasticity of categories: The case of colour. To appear in *British Journal of the Philosophy of Science.*
Branstetter, Katherine B.
1977 A reconstruction of Proto-Polynesian color terminology. *Anthropological Linguistics* 19:1–25.
Broch, Harald B.
1974 A note on the Hare color terms based on Brent Berlin and Paul Kay: Basic Color Terms. Their Universality and Evolution. *Anthropological Linguistics* 16(5):192–196.
Brown, Roger
1976 Reference. *Cognition* 4(2):125–153.
Brown, Roger W., and Eric H. Lenneberg
1954 A study of language and cognition. *Journal of Abnormal and Social Psychology* 49:454–462.
Bulmer, Ralph N. H.
1968 Karam colour categories. *Kivung* 1(3):120–133.
Burgess, Donald, Willett Kempton, and Robert E. MacLaury
1985 Tarahumara color modifiers: Individual variation and evolutionary change. In *Directions in Cognitive Anthropology.* J. W. D. Dougherty, ed., pp. 49–72. Urbana and Chicago: University of Illinois Press.

Burnham, R.W., and J.R. Clark
    1955 A test of hue memory. *Journal of Applied Psychology* 39:164–172.
Cairo, James E.
    1977 *The neurophysiological basis of basic color terms.* Ph.D. dissertation, SUNY, Binghamton.
Cairo, James E.
    1978 Dénomination des couleurs spectrales: Une théorie physiologique. In Tornay (1978a), pp. 39–70.
Callaghan, Catherine A.
    1979 Miwok color terms. *International Journal of American Linguistics* 45(1):1–4.
Caprile, Jean-Pierre
    1971 *La Dénomination des Couleurs chez les Mbay de Moïssala.* Bibliothèque de la SELAF 26. Paris: SELAF.
Caskey-Sirmons, Leigh A., and Nancy P. Hickerson
    1977 Semantic shift and bilingualism: Variation in the color terms of five languages. *Anthropological Linguistics* 19(8):358–367.
Chapanis, Alphonse
    1965 Color names for color space. *American Scientist* 53:327–346.
Cole, Michael, and Sylvia Scribner
    1974 *Culture and thought.* New York: Wiley and Sons.
Cole, Michael et al.
    1978 Cognition as a residual category in anthropology. In *Annual Review of Anthropology.* B. J. Siegel, A. R. Beals, and S. A. Tyler, eds., pp. 51–69. Palo Alto: Annual Reviews Inc.
Collier, George A.
    1973 Review of Basic Color Terms. *Language* 49(1):245–248.
Collier, George A. et al.
    1976 Further evidence for universal color categories. *Language* 52(4): 884–890.
Conklin, Harold C.
    1973 Color categorization: Review of Basic Color Terms, by Brent Berlin and Paul Kay. *American Anthropologist* 75(4):931–942.
Crane, Hewitt D., and Thomas P. Piantanida
    1983 On seeing reddish green and yellowish blue. *Science* 221:1078–1080.
Crawford, T. D.
    1982 Defining "basic color term." *Anthropological Linguistics* 24(3):338–343.
D'Andrade, Roy, and M.J. Egan
    1974 The color of emotion. *American Ethnologist* 1:49–63.
Derrig, Sandra
    1978 Metaphor in the color lexicon. In *Papers from the Parasession on the Lexicon, Chicago Linguistic Society.* D. Farkas, W. M. Jacobsen, and K. B. Todrys, eds., Chicago: Chicago Linguistic Society.
De Valois, Russell L., I. Abramov, and G. H. Jacobs
    1966 Analysis of response patterns of LGN cells. *Journal of the Optical Society of America* 56:966–977.
De Valois, Russell L., and Karen K. De Valois
    1975 Neural coding of color. In *Handbook of perception Vol. V: Seeing.* E. C.

Carterette and M. P. Friedman, eds., pp. 119–166. New York /
San Francisco / London: Academic Press.

De Valois, Russell L., and G. H. Jacobs
1968 Primate color vision. *Science* 162:533–540.

Dixon, R. M. W.
1976 Where have all the adjectives gone? *Studies in Language* 1:19–80.

Dougherty, Janet D.
1975 A universalist analysis of variation and change in color semantics.
Ph.D. dissertation, University of California, Berkeley.

Dougherty, Janet W. D.
1974 West Futuna color categories. Paper presented at the 73rd Annual
Meeting of the American Anthropological Association, Mexico
City.

Dougherty, Janet W. D.
1977 Color categorization in West Futunese: Variability and change.
In *Sociocultural Dimensions of Language Change*. B. G. Blount and
M. Sanches, eds., pp. 103–118. New York: Academic Press.

Dougherty, Janet W. D.
1978a On the significance of a sequence in the acquisition of basic colour
terms. In *Recent Advances in the Psychology of Language*. R. N. Campbell
and P. T. Smith, eds., pp. 133–148. New York / London: Plenum Press.

Dougherty, Janet W. D.
1978b Error types and their significance in children's responses. In *New
Approaches to Language Acquisition*. B. Ketteman and R. St. Clair,
eds., pp. 33–48. Tübingen: Günter Narr Verlag.

Dufort, Paul A., and Charles J. Lumsden
n.d. Color categorization and color constancy in a neural network
model of V4. University of Toronto: ms.

Durbin, Marshall
1972 Review of Basic Color Terms. *Semiotica* 6(3):257–278.

Egan, M.J., and Roy G. D'Andrade
n.d. The shape of color. Ms.

Ember, Melvin
1978 Size of color lexicon: Interaction of cultural and biological factors.
American Anthropologist 80:364–367.

Fijalkow, Jacques
1972 Généralisation du stimulus et de la réponse dans la formation des
concepts de couleur chez l'enfant. *Enfance* 5:361–378.

Fischer, Anne (ed.)
1970 *Current Directions in Anthropology*. Bulletins of the American Anthropological Association Vol. 3 (3): Part 2. Washington, D.C.: American
Anthropological Association.

Forbes, Isabel
1979 The terms brun and marron in modern standard French. *Journal of
Linguistics* 15:295–305.

Forbes, Isabel
n.d. The morphological patterning of basic colour terms in French. The
Queen's University, Belfast: ms.

Friedl, Erika
1979 Colors and culture change in Southwestern Iran. *Language in Society* 8:51–68.
Frisch, Jack A.
1972 Mohawk color terms. *Anthropological Linguistics* 14(8):306–310.
Fuld, K., J. S. Werner, and B. R. Wooten
1983 The possible elemental nature of brown. *Vision Research* 23:631–637.
Fuld, K., B. R. Wooten, and J. J. Whalen
1981 Elemental hues of short-wave and extraspectral lights. *Perception and Psychophysics* 29:317–322.
Garro, Linda
1986 Language, memory, and focality: A reexamination. *American Anthropologist* 88:128–136.
Gimpel, Mark
n.d. Notes on basic color terms (BCT) in Uto-Aztecan languages, and speculation on the BCT of Proto-Uto-Aztecan. University of California, Berkeley: ms.
Goethe, Johann W. von
1970 [1810] *Theory of Colors*. Cambridge, Mass.: MIT Press.
Greenfeld, Philip J.
1986 What is grey, brown, pink, and sometimes purple: The range of "wild-card" color terms. *American Anthropologist* 88:908–916.
Grossmann, Maria
1988 *Colori e Lessico: Studi sulla Struttura Semantica degli Aggettivi di Colore in Catalano, Castigliano, Italiano, Romeno, Latino e Ungherese*. Tübingen Beiträge zur Linguistik 310. Tübingen: Gunter Narr.
Hage, Per, and Kristen Hawkes
1975 Binumarien color categories. *Ethnology* 24:287–300.
Hamp, Eric P.
1980 Notes on Proto-Polynesian colours from K. B. Branstetter, A. L. 19: 1977. *Anthropological Linguistics* 22(9):390–391.
Hardin, Clyde L.
1988 *Color for Philosophers*. Indianapolis / Cambridge: Hackett Publishing Co.
Hardin, Clyde L.
n.d. Van Brakel and the not-so-naked emperor. To appear in *British Journal of the Philosophy of Science*.
Hardman, Martha J.
1981 Jaqaru color terms. *International Journal of American Linguistics* 47(1):66–68.
Harkness, Sara
1973 Universal aspects of learning color codes: A study in two cultures. *Ethos* 1(2):175–200.
Hays, David G., Enid Margolis, Raoul Naroll, and Dale Revere Perkins
1972 Color term salience. *American Anthropologist* 74(5):1107–1121.
Heider, Eleanor Rosch
1971 "Focal" color areas and the development of color names. *Developmental Psychology* 4(3):447–455.

Heider, Eleanor Rosch
    1972a Universals in color naming and memory. *Journal of Experimental Psychology* 93(1):10–20.
Heider, Eleanor Rosch
    1972b Probabilities, sampling and the ethnographic method: The case of Dani colour names. *Man* 7(3):448–466.
Heider, Eleanor Rosch, and Donald C. Olivier
    1972 The structure of the color space in naming and memory for two languages. *Cognitive Psychology* 3(2):337–354.
Heinrich, Albert C.
    1972 A non-European system of color classification. *Anthropological Linguistics* 14(6):220–227.
Heinrich, Albert C.
    1974 Color classification of some Central Canadian Eskimos. *Arctic Anthropology* 11(1):68–72.
Heinrich, Albert C.
    1978 Changing anthropological perspectives on color-naming behavior. *The Journal of Psychological Anthropology* 1(3):341–363.
Hering, Ewald
    1964 [1920] Outlines of a Theory of the Light Sense. Cambridge, Mass.: Harvard University Press.
Hickerson, Nancy P.
    1971 Review of Basic Color Terms. *International Journal of American Linguistics* 37(4):257–270.
Hickerson, Nancy P.
    1975 Two studies of color: Implications for cross-cultural comparability of semantic categories. In *Linguistics and Anthropology: In Honor of Carl F. Voegelin*. M. D. Kinkade, K. L. Hale and O. Werner, eds., pp. 317–330. Lisse: Peter De Ridder Press.
Hilbert, David R
    1987 *Color and Color Perception: A Study in Anthropocentric Realism*. Stanford: Center for the Study of Language and Information.
Hill, Jane H., and Kenneth C. Hill
    1970 A note on Uto-Aztecan color terminologies. *Anthropological Linguistics* 12(7):231–237.
Hunn, Eugene, and David French
    1977 Sahaptin color terms: A preliminary report. Paper presented at the Northwest Anthropology Conference, Victoria, B.C., April 1977.
Hurvich, Leo M.
    1981 *Color Vision*. Sunderland, Mass.: Sinauer.
Hurvich, Leo M., and Dorothea Jameson
    1957 An opponent-process theory of color vision. *Psychological Review* 64:384–404.
Ijima, Toshiro, Wolfgang Wenning, and Heinrich Zollinger
    1982 Cultural factors of color naming in Japanese: Naming tests with Japanese children in Japan and Europe. *Anthropological Linguistics* 24(2):245–262.

Jacobson-Widding, Anita
  1979 *Red-White-Black as a Mode of Thought*. Acta Universitatis Upsaliensis.
       Stockholm: Almqvist and Wiskell International.
Jernudd, Björn H., and Geoffrey M. White
  1983 The concept of basic color terms: Variability in For and Arabic.
       Anthropological Linguistics 25(1):61–81.
Johnson, Allen, Orna Johnson, and Michael Baksh
  1986 The colors of emotions in Machiguenga. *American Anthropologist*
       88:674–681.
Kay, Paul
  1970 [1966] Some theoretical implications of ethnographic semantics. In
       Fischer (1970), pp. 19–31.
Kay, Paul
  1973 Comments on N. B. McNeill's Colour and colour terminology.
       University of California at Berkeley, Language Behavior Research
       Laboratory.
Kay, Paul
  1975 Synchronic variability and diachronic change in basic color terms.
       Language in Society 4:257–270.
Kay, Paul
  1979 Interview on cognitive anthropology. In *On Going Beyond Kinship, Sex
       and the Tribe*. R. Pinxten, ed., pp. 31–37. Gent: Scientific Publishers.
Kay, Paul, Brent Berlin, and William R. Merrifield
  1975 *Human color categorization: A survey of the world's unwritten languages*.
       Research proposal submitted to the National Science Foundation.
Kay, Paul, Brent Berlin, and William R. Merrifield
  1979 *Human color categorization: A survey of the world's unwritten languages*.
       Research proposal submitted to the National Science Foundation
       (Renewal).
Kay, Paul, Brent Berlin, and William R. Merrifield
  1991 Biocultural implications of systems of color naming. *Journal of Lin-
       guistic Anthropology* 1(1):12–25.
Kay, Paul, and Willett Kempton
  1984 What is the Sapir-Whorf hypothesis? *American Anthropologist* 86(1):
       65–79.
Kay, Paul, and Chad K. McDaniel
  1978 The linguistic significance of the meanings of basic color terms.
       Language 54(3):610–646.
Kim, Andrew
  1985 Korean color terms: An aspect of semantic fields and related phe-
       nomena. *Anthropological Linguistics* 27(4):425–436.
Kinkade, M. Dale
  1988 Proto-Salishan Color. In *In Honor of Mary Haas*. W. Shipley, ed.,
       pp. 443–466. Berlin, New York, Amsterdam: Mouton de Gruyter.
Kristol, Andres M.
  1980 Color systems in Southern Italy: A case of regression. *Language*
       56(1):137–145.
Kuschel, Rolf, and Torben Monberg
  1974 'We don't talk much about colour here': A study of colour semantics
       on Bellona Island. *Man* 9:213–242.

Landar, Herbert J., Susan M. Ervin, and Arnold E. Horowitz
    1960 Navaho color categories. *Language* 36(3):368–382.
Lantz, DeLee, and Volney Stefflre
    1964 Language and cognition revisited. *Journal of Abnormal and Social Psychology* 69:472–481.
Lenneberg, Eric H.
    1953 Cognition in ethnolinguistics. *Language* 29:463–471.
Lenneberg, Eric H.
    1961 Color naming, color recognition, color discrimination: A reappraisal. *Perceptual and Motor Skills* 12:375–382.
Lucy, John A.
    1979 Whorf and his critics: Linguistic and nonlinguistic influences on color memory. *American Anthropologist* 81:581–607.
Lucy, John A., and Richard A. Shweder
    1988 The effect of incidental conversation on memory for focal colors. *American Anthropologist* 90:923–931.
Lumsden, Charles J.
    1985 Color categorization: A possible concordance between genes and culture. *Proceedings of the National Academy of Science of the U.S.A.* 82:5805–5808.
McClure, Erica
    1974 The acquisition and use of Spanish and English color terms among Mexican American children. Paper presented at the 73rd Annual Meeting of the American Anthropological Association, Mexico City.
McDaniel, Chad K.
    1972 *Hue perception and hue naming.* Honors thesis, Harvard College.
McDaniel, Chad K.
    1974 Basic color terms: Their neurophysiological basis. Paper presented at the 73rd annual meeting of the American Anthropological Association, Mexico City.
McDaniel, Chad K.
    n.d. Universals in color term semantics and their neurophysiological sources. Ms.
MacLaury, Robert E.
    1975 Reconstructions of the evolution of some basic color term lexicons: A step toward developing diachronic methods for testing the Berlin-Kay hypothesis. University of California, Berkeley: ms.
MacLaury, Robert E.
    1982 Prehistoric Mayan color categories. University of California at Berkeley, Language Behavior Research Laboratory: ms.
MacLaury, Robert E.
    1986a *Color in Mesoamerica Vol. I: A theory of composite categories.* Ph.D. Dissertation, University of California, Berkeley.
MacLaury, Robert E.
    1986b Color categorization in Shuswap, Chilcotin, Haisla, and Makah: A description. *Working Papers of the 21st International Conference on Salish and Neighboring Languages,* Seattle :100–122.
MacLaury, Robert E.
    1987a Color-category evolution and Shuswap yellow-with-green. *American Anthropologist* 89:107–124.

MacLaury, Robert E.
   1987b Coextensive semantic ranges: Different names for distinct van-
        tages of one category. In *Papers from the 23rd Annual Regional Meeting
        of the Chicago Linguistic Society.* B. Need, E. Schiller, and A. Bosch,
        eds., pp. 268–282. Chicago: Chicago Linguistic Society.
MacLaury, Robert E.
   1988a Information for comprehending Lillooet color data. Ms.
MacLaury, Robert E.
   1988b ProtoOtomanguean color categories. Paper presented at the 87th
        Annual Meeting of the American Anthropological Association,
        Phoenix.
MacLaury, Robert E.
   in press Exotic color categories: Linguistic relativity to what extent? *Jour-
        nal of Anthropological Linguistics* 1(1).
MacLaury, Robert E.
   in press Social and cognitive motivation of change: Measuring variabil-
        ity in color semantics. *Language* 67.
MacLaury, Robert E., and Brent D. Galloway
   1988 Color categories and color qualifiers in Halkomelem, Samish,
        Lushootseed, Nooksak, and Yakima. Paper presented at the 23rd
        International Conference on Salish and Neighboring Languages,
        Seattle.
MacLaury, Robert E., and Philip J. Greenfeld
   1984 How to say "blah" in fifty languages: A study of residual color
        categorization. Ms.
MacLaury, Robert E., Margot McMillen, and Stanley McMillen
   1979 Uspantec color categories: An experiment with field methods.
        Paper presented at the Ethnolinguistic Symposium of the IV
        Annual Mayan Workshop, Palenque, Chiapas, Mexico.
MacLaury, Robert E., and Stephen O. Stewart
   1984 Simultaneous sequences of color-category evolution. Paper presented
        at the 83rd Annual Meeting of the American Anthropological
        Association, Denver.
McManus, I. C.
   1983 Basic color terms in literature. *Language and Speech* 26:243–252.
McNeill, N. B.
   1972 Colour and colour terminology. *Journal of Linguistics* 8(1):21–33.
Maffi, Luisa
   1984 Somali colour terminology: An outline. In *Proceedings of the 2nd Inter-
        national Congress of Somali Studies. University of Hamburg, August 1–6,
        1983.* Vol. I: Linguistics and Literature, T. Labahn, ed., pp. 299–
        312. Hamburg: Helmut Buske Verlag.
Maffi, Luisa
   1988a World Color Survey Report. University of California, Berkeley: ms.
Maffi, Luisa
   1988b World Color Survey Typology. University of California, Berkeley:
        ms.
Maffi, Luisa
   1990 Cognitive anthropology and human categorization research: The
        case of color. University of California, Berkeley: ms.

Maffi, Luisa
in press Somali color term evolution: Grammatical and semantic evidence. *Anthropological Linguistics* 31.
Merrifield, William R.
1971 Review of Basic Color Terms. *Journal of Linguistics* 7(2):259–268.
Mervis, Carolyn B.
n.d. The acquisition of basic color terminology in English-speaking children. Cornell University: ms.
Mervis, Carolyn B., Jack Catlin, and Eleanor Rosch
1975 Development of the structure of color categories. *Developmental Psychology* 11:54–60.
Mervis, Carolyn B., and Eleanor Rosch
1981 Categorization of natural objects. In *Annual Review of Psychology*. M. R. Rosenzweig and L. W. Porter, eds., pp. 89–115. Palo Alto: Annual Reviews Inc.
Mervis, Carolyn B., and Emilie M. Roth
1981 The internal structure of basic and non-basic color categories. *Language* 57(2):384–405.
Meunier, Annie
1975 Quelques remarques sur les adjectifs de couleur. *Annales de l'Université de Toulouse* 11(5):37–62.
Meunier, Annie
1978 La couleur et ses termes en français. In Tornay (1978a), pp. 167–180.
Mills, Carl
1976 Universality and variation in the acquisition of semantic categories: English color terms. Paper presented at Nwave V, Georgetown University.
Mills, Carl
n.d. The acquisition of English color terms. University of Cincinnati: ms.
Mitsunobu, Meiyo
1972 Review of Basic Color Terms. *Studies in English Literature: English Literary Society of Japan* (March 1972):170–184.
Monberg, Torben
1971 Tikopia color classification. *Ethnology* 10(3):349–358.
Naroll, Raoul
1970 What have we learned from cross-cultural surveys? *American Anthropologist* 72(6):1227–1288.
Newcomer, Peter, and James Faris
1971 Review of Basic Color Terms. *International Journal of American Linguistics* 37(4):270–275.
Newton, Isaac
1979 [1730] *Opticks*. New York: Dover Publications Inc.
Nichols, Michael P.
1974 *Northern Paiute historical grammar*. Ph.D. dissertation, University of California, Berkeley.
Nichols, Michael P.
1980 Renewal in Numic color systems. In *American Indian and Indoeuropean*

Studies: Papers in Honor of Madison S. Beeler. K. Klar, M. Langdon, and S. Silver, eds., pp. 159–167. The Hague, Paris, New York: Mouton.

Nickerson, Dorothy, and Sidney M. Newhall
  1943 A psychological color solid. *Journal of the Optical Society of America* 33(7):419–422.

Osgood, Charles E., William H. May, and Murray S. Miron
  1975 *Cross-cultural universals of affective meaning.* Urbana / Chicago / London: University of Illinois Press.

Ottoson, D., and S. Zeki
  1985 *Central and Peripheral Mechanisms of Color Vision.* London: Macmillan.

Panoff-Eliet, Françoise
  1971 Compte rendu de Basic Color Terms. *L'Homme* 4:100–103.

Parra, François
  1978 Les bases physiologiques de la vision des couleurs. In Tornay (1978a), pp. 9–38.

Pollnac, Richard B.
  1972 *Variation in the cognition of Luganda color terminology.* Ph.D. dissertation, University of Missouri, Columbia.

Pollnac, Richard B.
  1975 Intra-cultural variability in the structure of the subjective color lexicon in Buganda. *American Ethnologist* 2(1):89–110.

Quinn, Paul C., B. R. Wooten, and Evette J. Ludman
  1985 Achromatic color categories. *Perception and Psychophysics* 37(3):198–204.

Raskin, L. A., S. Maital, and Marc H. Bornstein
  1983 Perceptual categorization of color: A life-span study. *Psychological Research* 45(2):135–145.

Ratliff, Floyd
  1976 On the psychophysiological bases of universal color terms. *Proceedings of the American Philosophical Society* 120(5):311–330.

Ratner, Carl
  1989 A sociohistorical critique of naturalistic theories of color perception. *Journal of Mind and Behavior* 10(4):361–372.

Rosano, J. L., B. R. Wooten, and P. C. Quinn
  1984 Evidence that brown is not an elemental color. Paper presented to the Optical Society of America, San Diego.

Rosch, Eleanor
  1973a On the internal structure of perceptual and semantic categories. In *Cognitive Development and the Acquisition of Language.* T. E. Moore, ed., pp. 111–144. New York: Academic Press.

Rosch, Eleanor
  1973b Natural categories. *Cognitive Psychology* 4(3):328–350.

Rosch, Eleanor
  1974 Linguistic relativity. In *Human Communication: Theoretical Explorations.* A. L. Silverstein, ed., pp. 95–121. New York: Halsted Press.

Rosch, Eleanor
  1975a Cognitive reference points. *Cognitive Psychology* 7:532–547.

Rosch, Eleanor
    1975b Cognitive representations of semantic categories. *Journal of Experimental Psychology-General* 104(3):192–233.
Rosch, Eleanor
    1975c Universals and cultural specifics in human categorization. In *Cross-cultural Perspectives on Learning.* R. W. Brislin, S. Bochner, and W. J. Lonner, eds., pp. 177–206. New York: Halsted Press.
Rosch, Eleanor
    1975d The nature of mental codes for color categories. *Journal of Experimental Psychology-Human Perception and Performance* 1:303–322.
Rosch, Eleanor
    1977 Human categorization. In *Studies in Cross-cultural Psychology* 1, N. Warren, ed., pp. 1–49. London: Academic Press.
Rosch, Eleanor
    1978 Principles of categorization. In *Cognition and Categorization.* E. Rosch and B. B. Lloyd, eds., pp. 27–48. Hillsdale: Laurence Erlbaum Associates.
Rosch, Eleanor, and Carolyn B. Mervis
    1975 Family resemblances: Studies in the internal structure of categories. *Cognitive Psychology* 7(4):573–605.
Rosch, Eleanor et al.
    1976 Basic objects in natural categories. *Cognitive Psychology* 8:382–439.
Royer, Francine
    1974 La terminologie des couleurs en montagnais. *Recherches Amèrindiennes au Quèbec* 4(2):3–16.
Sahlins, Marshall
    1976 Colors and cultures. *Semiotica* 16(1):1–22.
Saunders, B. A. C., and J. van Brakel
    1988 Re-evaluating Basic Color Terms. *Cultural Dynamics* 1(3):359–378.
Shields, Kenneth
    1979 Indo-European basic colour terms. *The Canadian Journal of Linguistics* 24(2):142–146.
Snow, David L.
    1971 Samoan color terminology: A note on the universality and evolutionary ordering of color terms. *Anthropological Linguistics* 13(8):385–390.
Stanlaw, James M.
    1987 *Color, culture, and contact: English loanwords and problems of color nomenclature in modern Japanese.* Ph.D. dissertation, University of Illinois, Champaign.
Steckler, Nicole A., and William E. Cooper
    1980 Sex differences in color naming of unisex apparel. *Anthropological Linguistics* 22(9):373–381.
Stefflre, Volney, Victor Castillo Vales, and Linda Morley
    1966 Language and cognition in Yucatan: A cross-cultural replication. *Journal of Personality and Social Psychology* 4:112–115.
Stephenson, Peter H.
    1972 The evolution of color vision in the Primates. *Journal of Human Evolution* 2:379–386.

Sternheim, C. E., and R. M. Boynton
    1966 Uniqueness of perceived hues investigated with a continuous judgmental technique. *Journal of Experimental Psychology* 72:770–776.
Suchman, Rosslyn Gaines
    1966 Cultural differences in children's color and form preferences. *Journal of Social Psychology* 70:3–10.
Sun, Richard K.
    1983 Perceptual distances and the basic color term encoding sequence. *American Anthropologist* 85:387–391.
Sun, Richard K.
    1984 Reply to Truex's comment on "Perceptual distances and the basic color term encoding sequence." *American Anthropologist* 84:695–699.
Swadesh, Morris
    1971 *The Origin and Diversification of Language.* Chicago/New York: Aldine/Atherton.
Thompson, Evan, Adrian Palacios, and Francisco J. Varela
    1991 Ways of coloring. To appear in *Behavioral and Brain Sciences.*
Tiffou, Étienne, and Yves C. Morin
    1982 Étude sur les couleurs en bourouchaski. *Journal Asiatique* 270(3–4):363–383.
Tornay, Serge
    1973 Langage et perception: La dénomination des couleurs chez les Nyangatom du Sud-Ouest éthiopien. *L'Homme* 12(4):66–94.
Tornay, Serge (ed.)
    1978a *Voir et Nommer les Couleurs.* Nanterre: Service de Publication du Laboratoire d'Ethnologie et de Sociologie Comparative de l'Université de Paris X.
Tornay, Serge
    1978b Introduction. In Tornay (1978a), pp. ix–li.
Tornay, Serge
    1978c L'étude de la dénomination des couleurs: Réflexion méthodologique. In Tornay (1978a), pp. 639–660.
Truex, Gregory F.
    1984 Comment on Sun. *American Anthropologist* 86:691–695.
Turton, David
    1978 La catégorisation de la couleur en mursi. In Tornay (1978a), pp. 347–368.
Turton, David
    1980 There's no such beast: Cattle and colour naming among the Mursi. *Man* 15(2):320–338.
Vallier, Dora
    1979 Le problème du vert dans le système perceptif. *Semiotica* 26(1/2):1–14.
Wald, Paul
    1978 Cloture sémantique, universaux et terminologie de couleur. In Tornay (1978a), pp. 121–138.
Wattenwyl, André von, and Heinrich Zollinger
    1978 The color lexica of two American Indian languages, Qechi and Misquito: A critical contribution to the application of the Whorf

thesis to color naming. *International Journal of American Linguistics* 44(1):56–68.

Wattenwyl, André von, and Heinrich Zollinger
1979 Color-term salience and neurophysiology of color vision. *American Anthropologist* 81:279–288.

Wattenwyl, André von, and Heinrich Zollinger
1981 Color naming by art students and science students: A comparative study. *Semiotica* 35:303–315.

Wescott, Roger W.
1970 Bini color terms. *Anthropological Linguistics* 13:251–252.

Wescott, Roger W.
1971 Proto-Indo-European color terms. *Language and Language Behavior Abstracts* (October 1971).

Wescott, Roger W.
1975a Tonal iconicity in Bini colour terms. *African Studies* 34(3):185–191.

Wescott, Roger W.
1975b Proto-Indo-Hittite color terms. In *Linguistics and Anthropology: In Honor of C. F. Voegelin.* D. M. Kinkade, K. L. Hale, and O. Werner, eds., pp. 691–699. Lisse: Peter de Ridder Press.

Whiteley, W. H.
1973 Colour-words and colour-values: The evidence from Gusii. In *Modes of Thought: Essays on Thinking in Western and non-Western Societies.* R. Horton and R. Finnegan, eds., pp. 145–161. London: Faber and Faber.

Wierzbicka, Anna
1990 The meaning of color terms: Cromatology and culture. *Cognitive Linguistics* 1(1):99–150.

Williams, Joseph M.
1976 Synaesthetic adjectives: A possible law of semantic change. *Language* 52(2):461–478.

Witkowski, Stanley R., and Cecil H. Brown
1977 An explanation of color nomenclature universals. *American Anthropologist* 79:50 57.

Witkowski, Stanley R., and Cecil H. Brown
1978 Lexical Universals. In *Annual Review of Anthropology* 7. B. J. Siegel, A. R. Beals, and S. A. Tyler, eds., pp. 427–451. Palo Alto: Annual Reviews Inc.

Witkowski, Stanley R., and Cecil H. Brown
1981 Lexical encoding sequences and language change: Color terminology systems. *American Anthropologist* 83:13–27.

Witkowski, Stanley R., and Cecil H. Brown
1982 Whorf and universals of color nomenclature. *Journal of Anthropological Research* 38(4):411–420.

Witkowski, Stanley R., and Harold W. Burris
1981 Societal complexity and lexical growth. *Behavioral Science Research* 16:143–159.

Wittgenstein, Ludwig
1977 *Remarks on Color.* Berkeley and Los Angeles: University of California Press.

Zimmer, Alf C.
    1982 What really is turquoise? A note on the evolution of color terms. *Psychological Research* 44(3):213–230.
Zisko, Sue
    1976 Phonetic symbolism in basic color terms. University of California, Berkeley: ms.
Zollinger, Heinrich
    1972 Human color vision: An interdisciplinary research problem. *Palette* 40:1–7.
Zollinger, Heinrich
    1976 A linguistic approach to the cognition of colour vision. *Folia Linguistica* 9(1/4):265–293.
Zollinger, Heinrich
    1979 Correlations between the neurobiology of colour vision and the psycholinguistics of colour naming. *Experientia* 35(1):1–8.
Zollinger, Heinrich
    1984 Why just turquoise? Remarks on the evolution of color terms. *Psychological Research* 46(4):403–409.

Index

Abraham, R. C., 84
Ainu, 27
Allen, G., 137–138, 141, 148
Anderson, P., 56
Aoki, H., 35, 89
Apache (Western), 21, 40, 43, 44, 45, 74
Arabic, 7, 27, 41, 90–91
Araucanian, 41
Arawak, 52–53
Arunta, 67–68
Aspillera, P. S., 100

Baganda, 53
Bagirmi, 63
Bambara, 53–54
Banfield, A. W., and J. L. MacIntyre, 34, 85–86
Bangi, 58
Bantu, 54
Bari, 38, 87
Bartlett, H. H., 74–75, 87–88, 97–98
Basic color terms. *See* Color terms, basic
Basso, K., 43, 74
Batak, 74–75
Battas, 41
Beaglehole, E., 73; and P. Beaglehole, 72
Bedauye, 83
Berber, 41, 44
Berlin, B., 10, 82, 162 (n13); and P. Kay, 94; and D. E. Breedlove and P. H. Raven, 161 (n4)
Bilingualism, as possible contaminant of data, 12
Bisayan, 41, 68–69, 169 (n9)
Black, M., and D. Metzger, 161 (n4)
Bleek, D. F., 75
Bohannan, P., 25, 60, 159 (n1), 161 (n8)

Boundaries of color categories, 13, 162 (n12)
Branstetter, K., 72, 163 (n14)
Brightness, 11, 24, 45, 49, 50, 53, 99, 104–112, 135, 138, 140, 147 149, 150, 163 (n16); "brightness dominated" color nomenclatures, 151; bright hues, 27; brightness and darkness, 50; low brightness, 107; maximum brightness, 105; middle brightness, 51; minimum brightness, 105
Bromley, M., 24, 25, 38, 47, 51
Brown, R., 138
Bulgarian, 7, 41, 91–92
Bullom, 54
Bulu, 55
Bushman, !Kung, 33, 75, 143

Canarese, 61
Cantonese, 7, 11–12, 21, 35, 40–42, 45, 92
Capell, A., 70–71
Catalan, 7, 35, 42, 92–93
Chafe, W., 162 (n10)
Chibcha, 79
Child's development of color vocabulary, 108–109
Chinook Jargon, 75–76
Chomsky, N., 109
Civilizations, complex, 16
Climate, possible effect on color terminology, 151
"Close to nature" peoples, 16
Collier, G., 82–83, 163 (n13)
Color blindness, 53
Color-blind tests, 25
Color categories, incipient. *See* Incipient color categories
Color category boundaries. *See* Boundaries of color categories

Prost, A., 81
Pukapuka, 72
Pyramid Wodo, 25, 51

Queensland, Fitzroy River, 29–31, 90
Queensland, Seven Rivers District, 27, 38, 58–59, 196

Rarotangan, 72
Rausch, P. J., 56–57
Ray, V. F., 149, 159 (n1)
Reconstruction, internal linguistic, of basic color terms, 36–41
Reinsch, 83
Relativity. *See* Linguistic relativity thesis
Ritual significance of color, 26, 57
Rivers, W. H. R., 27–28, 29, 30–31, 38–39, 41, 47–48, 51–52, 54, 58–59, 61, 62, 67, 69, 70, 134, 145–149, 163 (n14)
Robinson, C. H., 33, 84
Romney, A. K., 37
Russian, 21, 35, 36, 41, 98, 99; semantic relationships of *siniy* and *goluboy* in, 36; children's understanding of color terms, 109

Sáliba, 79
Samal, 21, 43–45
Samoyed, 41
Sapir, E., 2, 37
Saturation, 5, 8, 104–112
Segall, M. H., D. T. Campbell, and M. J. Herskovits, 134
Semantic theory, implications for, 13
Shona (Dialect A), 59, 62, 80, 160 (n2)
Shona (Dialect B), 59, 80
Siamese, 27, 41
Simon, K., 53, 59–60
Siwi (Siwa), 35, 89–90
Slobin, D., 98–99, 109
Smell, special lexical properties of, 13
Smith, E. W., 65
Somali, 63, 66–67
Songhai, 81
Spanish, 7, 32, 41, 69, 99
Spencer, B., and F. J. Gillen, 67–68
Stage I systems (BLACK, WHITE): 16, 17, 22, 23, 24, 25, 26, 38, 39, 46–52, 59, 69, 147
Stage II systems (BLACK, WHITE, RED): 16, 17, 18, 22, 24, 25–28, 30, 38, 40, 52–63, 65, 69, 105, 107, 143, 144, 146
Stage III systems: 15, 16, 17, 18, 28, 69, 76, 106, 107, 143

Stage IIIa systems (BLACK, WHITE, RED, GREEN): 18, 23, 28, 29, 63–67, 144
Stage IIIb systems (BLACK, WHITE, RED, YELLOW): 19, 23, 29, 30, 67–73, 144
Stage IV systems (BLACK, WHITE, RED, GREEN, YELLOW): 15, 18, 19, 21n, 23, 31–33, 38, 40, 42, 44, 45, 59, 73–83, 85, 88, 92, 96, 106–107, 144, 163 (n13)
Stage V systems (black, white, RED, green, YELLOW, blue): 19, 20, 21n, 23, 32, 33, 34, 38, 41, 42, 43, 44, 49, 83–87, 100, 106, 107
Stage VI systems (black white, RED, green, YELLOW, blue, brown): 19, 20, 23, 34, 35, 38, 44, 87–90, 98
Stage VII systems (eight, nine, ten, and eleven terms): 15, 16, 20, 22, 23, 35–36, 38, 40, 42, 44, 60, 90–104, 163 (n16)
Stapleton, W. H., 48, 55–56, 58, 59–60
Stems, analyzable and unanalyzable in linguistic internal reconstruction, 37
Stimuli, standardized: Figure 1, 5, 7, 82–83, 85, 103, 139, 160 (n3); acetate overlay, 5, 7, 162 (n13); acetate strips, 103; color chips, 5, 10, 13, 103, 139, 160 (n3); co-ordinate system, 11; light source, 162 (n3)
Stross, B., 42, 92, 99–100
Suffixes in formation of color terms, 29, 33, 51–52; importance in internal reconstruction, 38, 39, 40, 51, 52
Swahili, 7, 40, 58, 59–60
Synesthetic responses, 108
Syntax and phonology, biological foundations of, 109, 110

Tagalog, 7, 35, 41, 100–101
Tamil, 27, 33–34, 41, 61, 86–87
Tangma, 25
Tarascan, 33, 81–82
Taste, special lexical properties of, 13
Technological/cultural complexity, 16, 25, 104, 150
Temperate areas, possible effect of on color terminology, 151
Thai, 7, 10
Titchener, E. B., 147
Tiv, 26, 60, 159 (n1), 161 (n8)
Toda, 61
Tonga, 62
Tongan, 73